Religions and Beliefs

Series Editor: Ina Taylor

Islam

Musharraf Hussain
Anne Jordan

Nelson Thornes
a Wolters Kluwer business

Published in 2006 by:
Nelson Thornes Ltd
Delta Place
27 Bath Road
CHELTENHAM
GL53 7TH
United Kingdom

06 07 08 09 10 / 10 9 8 7 6 5 4 3 2 1

A catalogue record for this book is available from the British Library

ISBN 0 7487 9672 X

Edited by Judi Hunter
Picture research by Sue Sharp
Illustrations by Harry Venning and Angela Lumley
Page make-up by eMC Design

Printed in Croatia by Zrinski

Acknowledgements
With thanks to the following for permission to reproduce photographs and other copyright material in this book:

Cover photo: *Cherry Blossom Moon*, © 2006 Ayesha A. Mattu. All Rights Reserved. Used by Permission.

Alamy/ Roger Hutchings: 19 (Hadith 4); Alamy/ Sally & Richard Greenhill: 14A; ArkReligion.com/ Art Directors & Trip Photo Library/ Helene Rogers: 6B, 15E, 37C; Brand X RW (NT): 16B; Corbis/ Dennis Galante: 18 (Hadith 1); Corbis GS (NT): 12A(2); Corbis/ Kazuyoshi Nomachi: 5, 14B,C&D; Corbis/ Nic Bothma/ EPA files: 44A(2); Corbis/ Reuters: 61C; Corbis/ Stephen Hird/ Reuters: 40A; Corbis/ STScl/ NASA: 6A; Corel 173 (NT): 50A; Corel 219 (NT): 59C (top right); Corel 588 (NT): 57B; Corel 600 (NT): 12A(1); Corel 670 (NT): 59C (left); Digital Stock 11 (NT): 7D; Digital Vision 4 (NT): 9B; Digital Vision 7 (NT): 20A(1); Digital Vision 15 (NT): 52A; Empics/ AP: 60A; ePicscotland/ Ashley Coombes: 38A; Getty Images: 16A; Ingram ILG V2 CD4 (NT): 44A(1); Martin Sookias: 10A; Muslim Aid: 43; Muslim Hands: 48A, 49B; Muslim Youth Helpline: 36; Peter Sanders Photography: 15F, 26A, 31B, 32A, 46A; Photodisc 6 (NT): 21C; Photodisc 31 (NT): 53B; Photodisc 54B (NT): 34; Photodisc 38A (NT): 51B; Photodisc 73 (NT): 25; Rex Features/ EDPPICS/ D Bradley: 18/19 (Hadith 2); Rex Features/ Henryk T Kaiser: 19 (Hadith 5); Rex Features/ Jonathan Hordle: 28B; Rex Features/ Mark St George: 61B; Ronald Grant Archive: 22A; Ryan McVay/Photodisc 69 (NT): 19 (Hadith 3); Sally & Richard Greenhill: 7C, 35C&D; Stuart Sweatmore: 59C (bottom right); Science Photo Library/ Peter Menzel/ Dinamation: 20A(3); Tropix/ www.tropix.co.uk/ D Davis: 54A

The Muslim Youth Helpline for permission to use the information on pp.36–37.

Zahaid Malik for permission to use the information in 39C.

Comments on p.41 from a survey by the Muslim News.

Muslim Hands for permission to use the information on pp.48–49.

The IFEES for permissions to use the information on pp.54–55.

Every effort has been made to contact copyright holders. The publishers apologise to anyone whose rights have been inadvertently overlooked, and will be happy to rectify any errors or omissions.

Contents

 # Fast facts about Islam

Q *When did it begin?*

Muslims believe that humans have always been guided by God from the beginning of creation. They believe that God selected special people as prophets to teach his message. So throughout human history, Islam teaches, prophets have been telling the people of the world about God, for example Noah, Abraham, Moses and Jesus. All of them have taught the same message of surrendering to God's will, which is what Islam means. Some 1400 years ago the prophet Muhammad was sent by God, Muslims believe, to renew this old message.

Q *What is Islam?*

Islam is the name of the religion followed by Muslims. They believe that there is only one God and that people should surrender to God's will and follow the prophets.

Q *How many Muslims are there today?*

There are around 1.2 billion Muslims in the world today. Islam is the world's second largest religion, after Christianity. In the UK there are around 2.5 million Muslims. Not all of these actively follow their religion, but most would say that being a Muslim is an important part of who they are.

Q *Types of Islam*

There are two main sects of Muslims: Sunni Muslims and Shia Muslims. About 90 per cent of all Muslims are Sunni Muslims. Sunni and Shia Muslims share key beliefs about God and the Five Pillars. The division between the two groups occurred over who should lead the Muslim community in the years after Muhammad's death – a family line of rulers (Shia) or someone elected as the most worthy (Sunni).

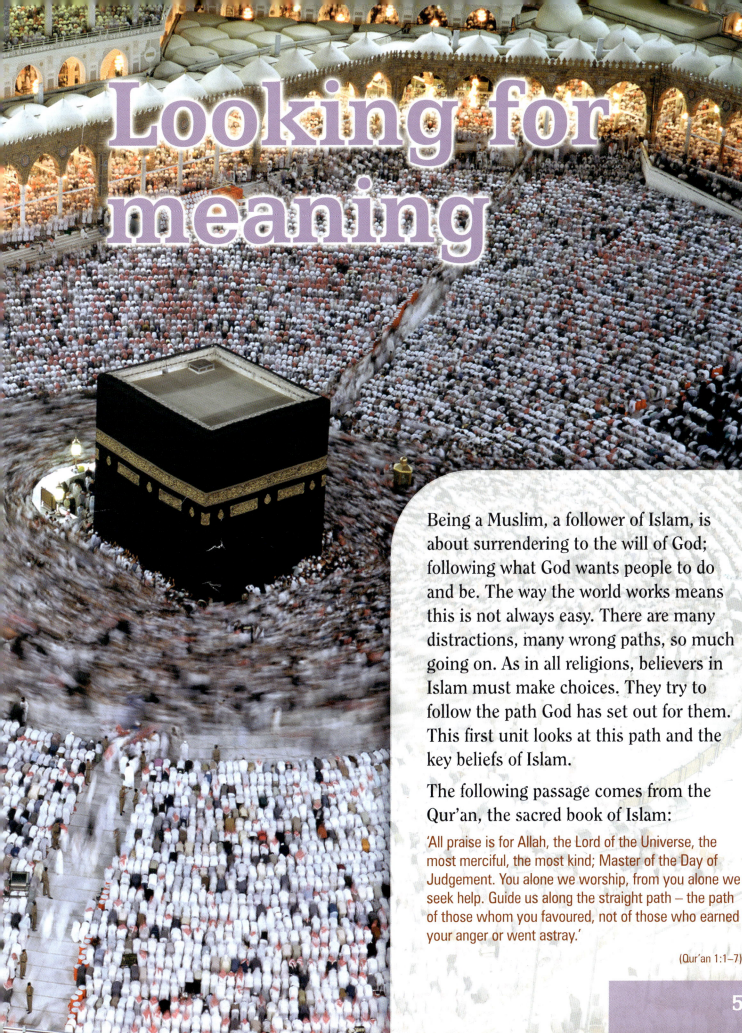

Looking for meaning

Being a Muslim, a follower of Islam, is about surrendering to the will of God; following what God wants people to do and be. The way the world works means this is not always easy. There are many distractions, many wrong paths, so much going on. As in all religions, believers in Islam must make choices. They try to follow the path God has set out for them. This first unit looks at this path and the key beliefs of Islam.

The following passage comes from the Qur'an, the sacred book of Islam:

'All praise is for Allah, the Lord of the Universe, the most merciful, the most kind; Master of the Day of Judgement. You alone we worship, from you alone we seek help. Guide us along the straight path – the path of those whom you favoured, not of those who earned your anger or went astray.'

(Qur'an 1:1–7)

5

Beliefs about God

A This photo shows a small part of our universe. How do you think the universe was created?

objective

to be able to describe what Muslims believe God is like and explain how Muslims relate to God

glossary

Allah
Atheist
Qur'an
Shahadah

God

Different people will have different answers to the question: 'Who created the universe?' A Christian may say 'God', a Hindu may say 'Krishna', an **atheist** may say that it is the result of a natural event and a Muslim will say that **Allah** created the universe. Allah is the Muslim name for God.

Muslims believe that God is:

- the creator of the universe
- the only god
- eternal
- all-powerful
- all-knowing
- all-seeing
- all-hearing
- all-willing.

What is God like?

Muslims believe that God is nothing like anything we know or understand. God doesn't have a body, or anything that can be seen or measured. God is not male or female (though God is called He in Islam). God was not born and will not die. God is outside time and space. God is simply beyond anything that humans can understand.

For Muslims, the belief that there is only one God, Allah, is so important that they give this belief a special name, the **Shahadah**. Everything in Islam rests on this one belief.

The first part of the Shahadah says, 'There is no God but Allah'. The second part of the Shahadah says, 'Muhammad is the Messenger of Allah'.

Read what the two Muslim teenagers on page 7 say about the Shahadah.

B The Shahadah.

1 Read this list again. Write down what you think each of the beliefs about God means.

C

For Muslims, it is very important to obey God's will because otherwise you are lost in life. The Prophet taught that anyone who believes that there is no God but Allah will be saved from hell.

D

For me, saying 'there is no God but Allah' doesn't just mean there's only one God. It means we shouldn't put anything but God first in our lives. Some people treat things like money or fame or being popular as more important than anything else. But God is the only thing worth worshipping.

Activity

2 The Shahadah states what is most important for Muslims in their lives. Is there *one* statement that could sum up what is really important to you in life? Write down this statement.

3 As a class, discuss what kinds of everyday things people today 'worship', which might stand in the way of what is actually really important.

How do we know about God?

The holy book of Islam is called the **Qur'an**. Muslims believe that the Qur'an contains God's actual words. Muslims believe that God chose the Prophet Muhammad as his messenger to reveal the Qur'an to people.

The descriptions of God in the Qur'an are called 'His Ninety-Nine Beautiful Names'. Some of the most frequent names for God in the Qur'an are: 'The Merciful'; 'Lord of the Universe'; 'The Generous'; 'The Forgiving'; 'The Patient'; and 'The Loving'.

For Muslims, the belief in God is personal and they put the love of God first in their lives. Muslims believe that God is with them all the time, and is very close. Muslims also believe that, 'God loves those who believe'. So there is a personal relationship with God.

'O Lord! We have been unjust to ourselves and if you do not forgive us and have mercy on us surely we will be losers.'

(Qur'an 7:23)

Activity

4 Describe in your own words *three* things Muslims believe about God.

5 What do you put first in your life? Explain why you have made this choice.

6 The Qur'an says that God is closer to people than 'their jugular vein'. Explain what you think this means about the sort of relationship Muslims have with God.

The Five Pillars of Islam

objective

to know what the Five Pillars are and explain how they help people know how to live their lives

glossary

Hajj
Makkah
Mosque
Ramadan
Salah
Sawm
Ummah
Zakah

A Why do Muslims call these five actions 'Pillars of Islam'?

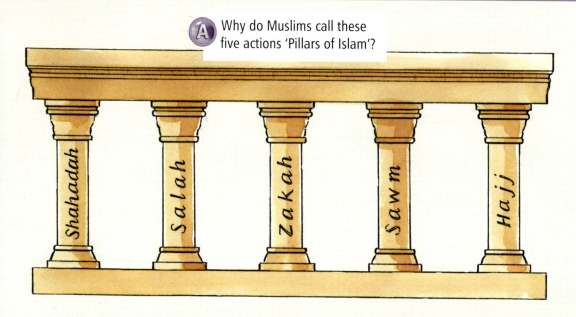

Muslims believe that when God decided to create humans, he said to the angels, 'I am placing on the earth one that shall be my deputy'. God has given humans a tremendous honour by making them his representatives on earth.

The angels were horrified because they saw humans' terrible potential for doing bad things as well as good. They couldn't understand why God should want such creatures and said, 'Will you put there one that will do evil and shed blood, when we have for so long sung your praises and glorified your name?'

Muslims believe that God has given humans a choice. They can choose to make sure God's will is done on earth, or ignore God's guidance. It is hard to know how to live up to such great responsibilities and Muslims believe God recognises this and has given humans his laws to follow. These include the Five Pillars of Islam on which all humans should try to build their lives.

The Five Pillars of Islam

Muhammad said, 'Islam is founded on five pillars: faith; regular prayer; almsgiving; fasting in Ramadan; and going on pilgrimage.'

The first pillar is the Shahadah.

Activity

1 a Look back to page 6 and write down the words of the Shahadah.

b What makes these words so important to Muslims?

The second pillar is regular prayer called **salah**. Muslims should pray five times a day at set times. This keeps God in their thoughts all through the day.

The third pillar is **sawm**. This is fasting during the month of **Ramadan**. Fasting involves not eating, drinking or smoking during daylight hours. When people think of food or water during fasting, they think of God. When they eat and drink again, they feel properly grateful to God for giving them the things needed to survive. This is why during the month of Ramadan Muslims give even more attention to worshipping God, such as additional prayers, going to the **mosque** more frequently and reading the whole Qur'an.

The fourth pillar, **zakah**, is almsgiving. Muslims should give at least 2.5% of their savings to help others each year. This is because Muslims believe wealth belongs to God and they have been trusted to spend it as God wishes.

Pilgrimage, called **Hajj**, is the fifth pillar. All Muslims should visit the holy city of **Makkah** once in their lifetime during the month of pilgrimage. On pilgrimage, people live pure lives devoted to God. Hajj is about getting as near as possible to the way God wishes humans to be. There is more about Hajj on pages 14–15.

Brothers and sisters

Muslims believe that God created the first humans, Adam and Eve, and that all the people born since then are their children. Therefore, we are all related like brothers and sisters of the same parents. Islam teaches that everyone is equal regardless of their colour, place of birth or wealth.

Anyone who is trying to follow God's path is a Muslim and Muslims across the world feel part of one huge family called the **ummah**.

Activity

2 Human life can be very complicated and distracting with a lot going on. Each pillar makes Muslims stop what they are doing and helps them to remember how God wants them to live. For a Muslim:

a what do you think are the most important things about being a human?

b how do each of the Five Pillars remind Muslims of God's wishes?

Activity

3 How different would your life be at school and in your neighbourhood if everyone acted like they were your brother or sister? Here are three situations to start you thinking:

- You have lost a favourite possession that a special person gave you.

- You have been asked to do something you think you should not do and want to ask someone's advice.

- You have too much fruit in your lunchbox and can't eat it all.

B Islam teaches that following God's path through life is like following a path to an everlasting waterhole through a dry, waterless desert.

Salah

Islam means surrendering to God's will. This doesn't mean just sitting back and letting things happen. Islam is about bringing everything people do into balance with God's will.

So Muslims try to stay aware of God all the time and build a strong relationship with him. Islam has many ways to help people with this. One way is through prayer – called salah. Muslims pray five times a day at set times linked to the movement of the sun.

Ahmed's blog

Hi, my name's Ahmed. I am 13. Since I was 10, I have prayed five times a day. This is what I did yesterday:

Ⓐ

| 6:45 am | Mum woke me up. I washed and prayed Fajr. Fajr is between first light of day and sunrise – really early in summer! |
| 8:35 am | Went to school. |

| 1:15 pm | Had lunch, washed, prayed Zuhr in school. Zuhr starts after the sun has passed directly overhead. |
| 3:30 pm | School ends. |

| 5:00 pm | Went to read the Qur'an. Prayed Asr in our mosque. Asr is between mid-afternoon and sunset. |

| 6:30 pm | Prayed Maghrib in the mosque. Maghrib is between sunset and the last light of day. |
| 7:00 pm | Dinner with the family. Helped Mum with the washing up. |

| 8:30 pm | Prayed Isha. Isha is between darkness and dawn. Helped my sister with her homework. |
| 10:30 pm | Went to bed after reciting a chapter of the Qur'an. |

B

Brings me closer to God.

Keeping to five daily prayers shows my obedience to God.

Praying five times a day means I can never forget God.

I can ask God for help.

Shows other people that I believe in God.

Why is salan important to me?

It's time out from everyday hassles.

It purifies my heart and mind.

C

Prayer is seen as a way of purifying the heart and mind. Muhammad once asked his followers this question: 'If they lived by a river and washed five times a day, would they be dirty?' Of course, his followers said, 'No'. Muhammad said the five daily prayers do the same thing. They remove sins from the heart.

A strong relationship

The daily prayers are about remembering how important God is to all things and thanking him for showing people how they should behave. Everything about the prayers is designed to help people remember their responsibilities to God. For example:

- Before they pray, Muslims must prepare themselves by washing. This is called **wudu**. This reminds people that they are bringing their whole body to worship God.
- Special body movements during prayers help emphasise what the prayers mean. At one point, people kneel and touch their heads to the ground. This reminds people to love God more than they love themselves.
- Every Friday, men are expected to visit their mosque for the midday prayer. This special day and time of prayer underlines the importance of setting time aside throughout the week to remember responsibilities to God.

Muslims can pray at any time of day – salah is just the minimum. Many people make personal prayers after the daily prayers. These might be to ask God for help with a problem, or to say sorry for something they have done wrong.

1 Read Ahmed's reasons why salah is important to him in **B**. Explain:

   a how praying five times each day shows obedience

   b why Ahmed says praying brings him closer to God

   c what Ahmed means by 'purifies my heart and mind'.

2 Read Ahmed's blog page in **A**. Praying five times a day is a big commitment. How would you feel about giving up all this time each day? How do you think Ahmed would answer this question? You can check your answers with Ahmed: e-mail him at islam@nelsonthornes.com

3 Draw a spider diagram to show the different ways prayer helps Muslims stay close to God in their lives.

4 Islam teaches that 'prayer is better then sleep'. Write *three* reasons on a post-it note explaining why Ahmed should wake up early to pray. Ahmed can stick this on his alarm clock to remind him why it's important to get up early!

Life after death

In Islam, God gives humans a choice. They can believe in him or they can deny his existence. If humans choose to believe in God, then the purpose of their life is to do good by following God's path. The purpose of death is to test whether people have lived a good life or not. The Qur'an says:

'He created life and death in order to test which of you does good works.'

(Qur'an 67:2)

Islam teaches that humans are made of a physical body and a non-physical **soul**. When a person dies, the soul lives on whilst the body turns to dust. The soul is waiting for the Day of Judgement and this wait can be pleasant or painful according to the life the person has lived. The Qur'an says:

'To Allah we belong and to Him we are returning.'

(Qur'an 2:156)

Activity

1 We all face many choices every day, and sometimes it is hard to know which choice to make.

a Think about someone you know who always seems to know what he or she is going to do next with his or her life. Why do you think some people find making choices easier then others?

b How do you think a Muslim would make decisions about how to live their life?

A Some Muslims believe the soul is questioned in the grave and sent to somewhere like a garden, or somewhere like a dungeon.

The Day of Judgement

Muslims believe the Day of Judgement is a fixed day in the future. The universe will come to an end and everything in it will be completely destroyed. Everyone who has ever lived will be **resurrected** and brought to stand before God, to account for all that they did in their life. Then the judgement will begin. Islam teaches that everyone will wait anxiously for God's decision. Everyone's deeds will be weighed in the scales of justice. Those who followed the ways of God will be rewarded with paradise, and those who denied the existence of God will be sent to hell.

Paradise

The Qur'an says that paradise is so magnificent and amazing that 'no one can imagine what delight awaits for them as a reward for their works'. Muhammad described paradise like this:

'Its walls will be gold coated, the floor coverings of pearls and rubies, it will have every kind of luxury and comfort imaginable. The people of paradise will never get old nor will they ever die.'

(Hadith)

> **Activity**
>
> 2 Muslims believe that God has fixed our time of death and we cannot do anything to lengthen our life. Every day could be the last day on earth so Muslims should live every day as if it is their last.
>
>   a What difference would it make to your life if you lived every day like it was your last on earth?
>
>   b What things would you make sure you did or said?
>
>   c What things might you not bother doing, or avoid completely?

Hell

The Qur'an says,

'Fear the fire of hell, whose fuel is people… who disbelieve.'

(Qur'an 2:24)

Muslims believe that hell is a place of torture and suffering. The intensity of the fire of hell is so severe that if a hole the size of a needle's head was opened from hell into this world, then it would burn everything on earth.

> **Activity**
>
> 3 A website on beliefs in life after death has made some serious mistakes about Muslim beliefs. Finish off this email to the website, pointing out their mistakes.

Send Now   Send Later

To: help@myh.org.uk
Cc:
Attachments:

I am writing to point out two serious mistakes in what your website says about Muslim beliefs on life after death.

The website says 'Muslims believe when you die you are resurrected if you have led a good life'. This is wrong because…

The website says 'Islam teaches that only those who have done no wrong will go to paradise'. This is not correct because…

Hajj

Photo **A** shows a Muslim family at home. On the wall behind them is a picture of the **Ka'bah** Mosque. It is a central image for Muslims and found in most Muslim homes and businesses.

A

The Ka'bah

Muslims believe the Ka'bah stands on the site of the first ever place of worship, built by the first man, Adam. It was then rebuilt by the Prophet Ibrahim. In Muhammad's time, the temple was used for worshipping many different gods. It contained 350 idols. Muhammad broke up all these idols and returned it to the worship of God alone.

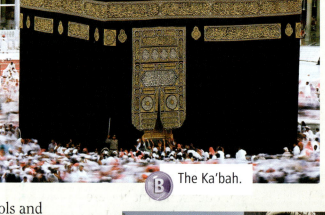
B The Ka'bah.

Every mosque around the world shows the direction of the Ka'bah because Muslims face it when they pray. This is because the Ka'bah is called God's house and reminds Muslims that God needs to be central to their lives if they are to avoid sin.

Pilgrims on Hajj walk around the Ka'bah seven times praying. This is to show their love for God and dedication to him. The Ka'bah stands for God being at the centre of Muslims' lives.

C Al-Hajar al-Aswad – the special stone.

Photo **C** shows a special stone in the wall of the Ka'bah, which Muslims believe was sent down to earth by God. It stands for the gifts God has given humans. Pilgrims cheer as they pass it, or try to kiss it or touch it if they are close enough.

D Pilgrims putting on **ihram**.

Ihram

On pilgrimage, people wear simple robes so that all signs of wealth and culture are removed (Photo **D**). This helps all Muslims to feel equal and united. Instead of thinking about themselves, they focus on living as God wills. These special clothes are taken home after Hajj. Some people will ask to be buried in them.

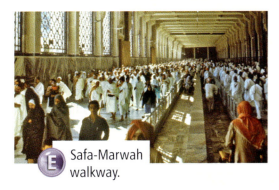

 Safa-Marwah walkway.

Safa-Marwah

Pilgrims run up and down a long walkway (Photo **E**) to follow the journey of the Prophet Ibrahim's wife, Hajar. Hajar and her son Isma'il were left in the desert at God's mercy. They had no water and Hajar ran desperately between two hills searching for water as she knew God would provide for them. The water appeared at a spot now called the Zamzam. The water stands for God, who is like water for those dying of thirst and will provide what is needed to survive.

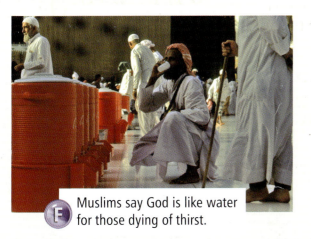

Muslims say God is like water for those dying of thirst.

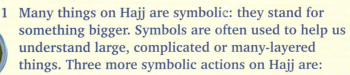

1 Many things on Hajj are symbolic: they stand for something bigger. Symbols are often used to help us understand large, complicated or many-layered things. Three more symbolic actions on Hajj are:

- the standing
- throwing stones at pillars
- sacrificing a goat.

Read the following information. Which statements link together to explain the meaning behind the three symbolic actions?

I The most important action on pilgrimage is the 'staying at the Plain of Arafat'. Pilgrims go to a place called Arafat and stand in silent prayer under the hot desert sun, often for many hours.

2 Pilgrims throw stones at the white pillars.

3 A goat is usually sacrificed at the end of the pilgrimage. Part of the meat is given to the poor.

A God tested Ibrahim by telling him to sacrifice his son, Isma'il. On their way to the sacrifice, Satan tried three times to persuade them to disobey God. Such was their faith in God that both father and son obeyed God without question and threw stones at Satan. At each spot a pillar of stone appeared. God stopped Ibrahim just as he was preparing to kill his son and a ram was sacrificed instead.

B Muhammad asked God to forgive the sins of all those who 'stand' at Arafat.

C Muslims should submit to God's will, come what may.

D On the Day of Judgement, all people will stand before God to be judged. Those who have ignored the will of God will be sent to the flames of hell.

E God wishes people to share their worldly goods with those who are less fortunate.

2 'Hajj has changed my life,' said 65-year-old Yusuf. 'I wish I had been able to go earlier in my life.' Explain what Yusuf meant when he said this. Think about:

- why Hajj is important for Muslims?
- how the actions of Hajj have made such an impact on Yusuf?
- what might have stopped Yusuf going on Hajj earlier?

3 The Ka'bah is a very simple building: a cube made of plain stone. Around it is the most magnificent mosque, yet it is the simple Ka'bah that is the centre of Islam. Explain what this tells you about how Muslims view their religion and God.

The Qur'an

objective

to be able to describe what is in the Qur'an and explain why it is important for Muslims

glossary

Bible
Surah
Torah

Muslims believe that humans should choose to believe in God and live according to his will. The holy book of Islam, the Qur'an, helps Muslims to know what is the will of God. It is the first source of authority for Muslims because it is believed to have come directly from God. This means it is something Muslims believe they can trust to guide their journey through life.

In Islam, the Qur'an is believed to be the actual words of God. Over centuries, God had given messages to different prophets, like the prophets recorded in the **Torah** and **Bible**. In the Qur'an, 25 prophets are named including Adam, Abraham, Moses, David and Jesus. Muslims believe the Qur'an was God's final and complete message, which was given to the last prophet, Muhammad.

The story of the Qur'an

Muhammad often went to a cave near his home city of Makkah to worship God. One time, as he sat lost in worship, he heard a voice outside the cave say, 'Read!' Muhammad said, 'I cannot read'. The voice again said, 'Read!' and Muhammad gave the same answer. After the third time the voice said:
'Read, in the name of your Lord who creates;
Created man from a clot.
Read, and it is your Lord the most bountiful,
who teaches by the pen,
Teaches man that which he knows not.'

Muslims believe that this is the first revelation of the Qur'an. It happened during the month of Ramadan in 610 CE.

When Muhammad looked outside the cave, into a bright beam of light, he saw a likeness of a man who said, 'Muhammad, you are God's messenger and I am Jibril the Angel'. This was the beginning of the revelation of the Qur'an, which continued for the next 23 years until Muhammad's death in 632 CE.

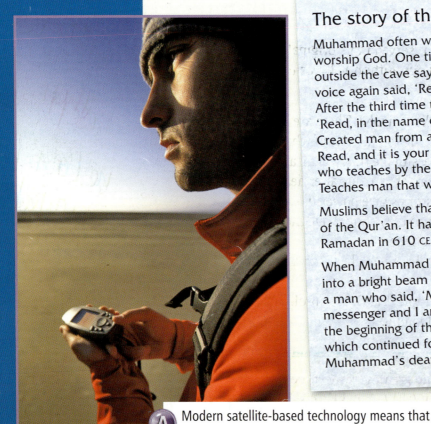

A Modern satellite-based technology means that explorers can be absolutely sure where they are on their journey. Muslims believe the Qur'an is the most accurate and reliable guide for the most important journey of all.

B As the moon and stars guided travellers at night across the desert, so the Qur'an is a guide for Muslims throughout their lives.

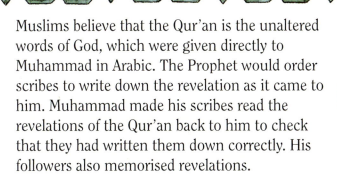

Muslims believe that the Qur'an is the unaltered words of God, which were given directly to Muhammad in Arabic. The Prophet would order scribes to write down the revelation as it came to him. Muhammad made his scribes read the revelations of the Qur'an back to him to check that they had written them down correctly. His followers also memorised revelations.

The first authenticated copy of the Qur'an was available within two years of Muhammad's death. Copies of this original version were made and sent to the major cities of the Islamic world. Two of these copies still exist.

1 Do you know anything by heart – maybe a poem or song lyrics? Why did you choose to remember it like this?

2 Explain why Muslims believe that the words in the Qur'an are the actual words of God.

The teachings of the Qur'an

Muslims believe that the Qur'an has been preserved in its original form. It has not been changed. Therefore, it commands authority. It has to be obeyed.

The Qur'an is divided into 114 chapters, called **surahs**. There are four main themes running through the Qur'an as a guide to Muslims of what to believe and how to live a peaceful and successful life that will please God.

- Beliefs about the unseen: about God, prophets and life after death.
- Stories about the prophets. These vivid stories give powerful examples of how people should behave and what values they should live their lives by, such as generosity, forgiveness and patience.
- Teachings on how to worship God through prayer, charity and pilgrimage.
- Rules for living as good citizens. For example, the Qur'an prohibits drinking alcohol, gambling, stealing and killing.

3 Muslims treat the Qur'an with the greatest respect, believing it contains the actual words of God. Imagine that a UK charity has asked you to write a leaflet to explain to its workers why the Qur'an is so important. This will go out to all charity staff working in Muslim communities.

Sunnah: The way of Muhammad

glossary

Ahadith
Hadith
Sirah
Sunnah

Muslims believe that the Qur'an is the final book from God received by Muhammad. It is the first source of authority for Muslims. The Qur'an gives general orders and principles, but not details of how to put the will of God into practice. When he was teaching, Muhammad would explain and give more details. He would show people how to put God's commands into practice. This is called **Sunnah**, which means 'the practical example', 'the way'. In the Qur'an, God says,

'In the life of the prophet there is a beautiful example for you to follow'.

(Qur'an 33:21)

Muhammad's disciples wrote down what Muhammad did and said. This record of the Sunnah is called the **Hadith** (plural = **Ahadith**). It is the second source of authority for Muslims.

Hadith 1

'A man came to the Prophet and asked, "Who, among all people, is most worthy of my good company?" The Prophet replied, "Your mother." The man asked, "Who next?" The Prophet said, "Your mother." The man asked again, "Who next?" Again, the Prophet said, "Your mother." Only next did he say, "Your father."'

Hadith 2

'The Prophet once said, "There was a traveller passing through a desert. He was thirsty. When he came to a well he went down into the well and drank to his heart's content. Then he saw a dog licking the wet sand around him. He went down into the well again and filled his moccasin with water and gave the dog a drink. God thanked the man."'

Activity

1 Explain the differences between the Qur'an and the Ahadith.

2 a Who do you look up to in life? What impresses you about what they do and say?

   b Write your hero's name and *three* things you really like about the way they live their lives.

   c Write *three* things you could do in your life to be more like your hero.

Hadith 3

'The Prophet said, "Every good action is a charity. For example, smiling at your friend when you see him."'

Hadith 4

'A man once asked Muhammad, "What's the best thing in Islam?" He replied, "To feed people and pleasantly greet everyone whether you know them or not."'

Hadith 5

'Muhammad said, "You are not a true believer until you love for your brother or sister what you love for yourself."'

Activity

3 a Read the five Ahadith shown here carefully and thoughtfully.

   b Explain what each Hadith is teaching about how people should behave towards each other and towards animals.

4 A Muslim TV company has a popular 'soap' about life in a farming village. They want to write an episode that features each of the five Ahadith shown here. Write the outline plot for this episode. You must make sure that you do not include any actions that would upset the company's Muslim viewers.

5 Which of these five Ahadith do you think is the most important? Explain the reason for your choice.

There are various traditional biographies of Muhammad called **sirah**. Muslims read these to find out more about his life. Muslims believe that these biographies are, for the most part, accurate portrayals of Muhammad and act as guides on how to follow his example.

Activity

6 Using the Internet find one of the stories about Muhammad as a child. Then write up the story so that it could be told to a young child. Remember to include what the story teaches about how to be a good Muslim.

19

Believing the truth

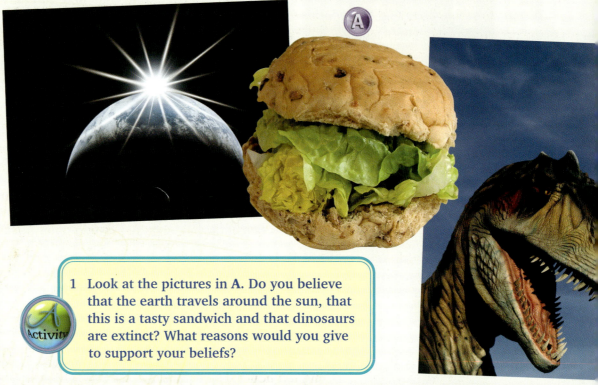

objective

to be able to describe Muslim views on truth and religion and explain your own views on what is true and what you trust

glossary

Jinn

Ⓐ

Activity

1 Look at the pictures in **A**. Do you believe that the earth travels around the sun, that this is a tasty sandwich and that dinosaurs are extinct? What reasons would you give to support your beliefs?

There are different reasons for believing that something is true. Films make dinosaurs look very real but we don't just believe our eyes because we trust scientific evidence that dinosaurs are extinct. You probably believe that the earth travels around the sun, even though you've never seen it happen for yourself. Yet, centuries ago, people believed the sun travelled around the earth. Scientists discovered the truth through careful observation, thinking and experiments, and used their findings to convince everyone else. However, some things we need to discover for ourselves, for example, what sandwiches taste best to us.

Muslims believe that there are three sources of knowledge about the world and religious truth as to why we should believe in God. These are:
- the prophets of God
- the human intellect
- the five senses.

The first two sources are most important when talking about religious truth. Some religions have a long tradition of arguments to prove that God exists, and what God is like. Islam does not go into such in-depth discussion because Muslims believe God is beyond any human understanding or classification.

However, Muslims believe that God has given humans the ability to reason, to think and to know. Muslim philosophers (called mutakkalimum) used this brain power to prove the existence of God (**B**).

Ⓑ

Nothing comes from nothing
But the universe exists.
So how did the universe come from nothing?
There must be something that made the universe happen.
That something is God.

Signs of God

Muslims believe that there are signs that God exists all around them: the beautiful sunset; the winds blowing the clouds; and the growth of lush green vegetation. The Qur'an often points out that the wonderful things in nature are clear evidence of God's creation, power and majesty, as how could they have come about if not by God's will? The Qur'an says,

'In the creation of the heavens and the earth and in the alteration of day and night, these are signs for people of understanding.'

(Qur'an 3:191)

2 a **Explain in your own words how Islam looks to prove the existence of God. What questions does this argument raise?**

   b **The Qur'an teaches that the awesome beauty of the natural world is proof of God's existence. How might a non-religious person explain why humans find the natural world so beautiful and impressive?**

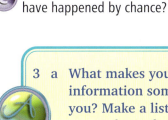

C Could such a beautiful world have happened by chance?

The prophets of God

Islam teaches that God is the guide for people to live a lifestyle that is pleasing to him. Muslims believe that God has sent prophets to tell people his message. The prophets were truthful, honest, amazing people chosen by God. God inspired them and they spoke to him. They were great teachers. They were able to see the unseen world and things no one else could see: angels; **jinn**; heaven; and hell. Muslims believe that the messages passed on by the prophets can be trusted.

Muslims believe in all of the prophets mentioned in the Bible, including Jesus. But Muslims believe that God's messages through these prophets were not always recorded properly and accurately. So Jesus, for example, would never have claimed to be God in human form. For Muslims, some of Jesus' disciples made up this claim when they were writing about Jesus after his death.

In Islam, the last and greatest prophet was Muhammad. Through Muhammad, God made his message perfect and Muslims have taken great care that the message recorded in the Qur'an has never changed over the centuries.

3 a **What makes you trust the information someone gives you? Make a list of things to watch out for if you want to know if someone is telling the truth.**

   b **What qualities did the prophets have that made their messages trustworthy?**

   c **From what you know about Islam and Christianity, what do you think Muslims and Christians would agree on about Jesus? What would they disagree about?**

Islam and science

Science and religion often seem to be two very different things. Some say science is about experiments and proof; religion is about worship and belief.

A In the 1991 film *Robin Hood: Prince of Thieves*, Morgan Freeman plays Azeem, a Muslim who knows far more about science and medicine than the English Christians. This is historically accurate – the European Crusaders were amazed by the scientific and technological advances of the Muslims societies of the Middle East.

Muslims believe that there is no conflict between scientific truth and their religious beliefs. The Qur'an tells people 'to observe', 'to think', 'to reflect' and 'to understand'. Muslims see science as a tool from God to help them to understand the universe that God has created. So Muslims have always been great scholars and scientists.

Muslim scholars made new discoveries in maths, physics, medicine, astronomy and chemistry long before the medieval Christians. Muslim scholars laid the foundation of modern science. We use many Arabic words in maths and science. For example, algebra, chemistry and zero are all Arabic words.

1 Between the twelfth and seventeenth centuries, Muslim scholars led the way in science. Design a poster to advertise the Muslim discoveries and achievements of this period.

825 CE	835 CE	840 CE
 Jabir Ibn Hayyam discovers nitric acid and refines techniques of crystallisation and distillation.	$0\ 1\ 2\ 3\ 4$ $5\ 6\ 7\ 8\ 9$ Al Khwarizimi introduces zero and Arabic numerals.	$x + y = xy$ Al Khwarizimi develops algebra, linear and quadratic equations.

B

Islam and the Big Bang

The Qur'an teaches that God created the universe and everything in it in six days. Before the universe was created, there was nothing. Modern science puts forward the **Big Bang** theory, in which everything was created in an instant. While some modern scientists would argue that the universe was created in this way by chance, Muslim scientists believe God caused the Big Bang. They would say that since science teaches that creating something out of nothing is impossible, only God makes sense as an answer to the Big Bang theory. Only God can do the impossible.

Muslims would not disagree that the universe developed over many billions of years. Although the Qur'an says that it was created in six days, the six 'days' could mean six 'long periods of time', extending over billions of years.

Islam and evolution

Charles Darwin's theory of **evolution** explains how life on our planet has come to be so varied and well-adapted to its surroundings. Muslims would not entirely agree with this theory, as the Qur'an teaches that God made all creatures in their final form. All humans are descendants of Adam and Eve, rather than evolving from apes. In Islam, humans are God's most important creation. For Muslims, the marvellous variety and intricate perfection of the natural world is a sign of God's creative power.

The Qur'an says of God:

'Do they not see how God started the creation and then reproduces it? That is easy enough for God.'

(Qur'an 29:19)

This means God initiated the process of creation and continues to change and reproduce it.

2 a Explain why the Big Bang theory does not necessarily come into conflict with Islam's teachings on the creation of the universe.

b Explain why the theory of evolution comes into conflict with Islam's teachings about life on earth.

3 The great English scientist Isaac Newton once said that all his discoveries counted for very little compared with what was still unknown. He described his life's work as having been like a boy playing with pebbles in front of a vast ocean.

Do you agree that there are still things to discover, or has science answered questions without the need to believe in God?

975 CE	1020 CE	1030 CE
Muwattaq publishes a book containing 585 remedies and drugs.	Al Haytham publishes a classic *Book of Optics*, which is later used by European scientists Da Vinci and Kepler.	Ibn Sina writes a medical textbook called *Qanun* which remains an important medical book in Europe from the twelfth century to the seventeenth century.

Assessment for Unit 1

> In the name of God, Most Gracious, Most Merciful
>
> Praise be to God, the Cherisher and Sustainer of Worlds,
> Most Gracious, Most Merciful,
> Master of the Day of Judgement.
>
> You do we worship, and Your aid we seek,
> Show us the straight way,
> The way of those on whom You have bestowed Your Grace,
> Those whose (portion) is not wrath,
> And who go not astray.
>
> Al-Fatihah, 'The Opening' (Surah 1)

These questions test different sets of skills in RE. Which skills do you need to work on? Choose the level you need and work through the tasks set.

Level 3

- What is the name of the holy book of Islam?
- Why do you think all Muslims learn to read this book in Arabic?
- Write out the passage here in your own words. Describe what it says God is like and what God can do.
- Muslims believe God has set out a path for them to follow in their lives. What things guide you in your life. Why do you follow these guides?

Level 4

- Describe *three* sources of authority a Muslim could turn to if they wanted to know what was right or wrong.
- Choose another religion and give *three* sources of authority a believer could turn to.
- What *three* sources of authority would you turn to if you wanted to know something? Explain which you value most, and why.

Level 5

- Describe what Muslims believe will happen after they die.
- Christianity, Judaism and Islam all teach that there will be a Day of Judgement, and that believers should live as though each day could be the Day of Judgement. What would the impact of this be on believers, and how would things be different for someone from a religion that does not have a Day of Judgement, or a Humanist?
- What is your view of life after death? How much do you think your view has been influenced by any particular religious or non-religious beliefs?

Level 6

- Professor Fred Hoyle said that the chances of a planet 'happening' to have the right conditions for human life were as likely as a hurricane passing through a scrap yard and creating a jumbo jet. What reasons could he give for the existence of life on earth? How convincing do you find his hurricane argument? How would you explain the existence of life on earth?

Who is responsible?

In Islam, every person has a choice. If they choose to be a Muslim, they have a great responsibility to live according to God's will.

We all face choices all the time and sometimes it is difficult to know what to do, how to behave, who to follow. Muslims believe God has shown people the way through all these problems, through the lives of the prophets and in the Qur'an.

Islam teaches these values, so that people can apply them in their own lives and try to live up to them. A key value is thinking of others above yourself. This means being kind, generous, considerate and respectful. People also have responsibilities to themselves as representatives of God. They should be patient and modest and stop themselves from getting angry.

Muslims also have the responsibility of looking after anyone who comes to them for help, or as a guest. They should not sit and wait to find ways to show they are following God's will. They should go out and find ways to help people.

Lifestyle: choices and effects

objective

to explain how Muslims make choices and to give your own views and advice on conflicts British Muslims might face between their religion and culture and the society they live in

glossary

Hadith
Qur'an

Western countries, like the UK, are not always easy places to be a Muslim. Some countries around the world are Muslim countries and here everything is set up to help Muslims live according to God's will. For example, alcohol is not permitted in Islam, so in Saudi Arabia it isn't available. But this isn't the case in the UK.

Also, parts of Western cultures have some conflicts with Muslim teachings. For example, in Islam people are expected to dress modestly. This can conflict with Western fashions that show a lot of flesh!

Growing up is pretty tough, with lots of choices to make about what type of person to be and what kind of lifestyle to lead. It helps if you have a clear idea of what sort of person you want to be, but, even then, it can be confusing because you never know what effect your choices will have on your future.

Activity

Read through the dilemmas (problems) in **B** which Muslim teenagers have sent in to a problem page in a magazine called 'UK Islam Today'. The magazine has a religious expert who gives a relevant teaching for each problem. You have been called in as a consultant on teen issues in the UK today. Your job is to put together the teaching and the problem and come up with some good advice for the teenagers to follow.

A Is the UK an easy place to be a Muslim?

Dilemma 1

I find praying five times a day difficult because no one else in my school does it. When I was on holiday this year it was great. We were in a Muslim country (Saudi) and people just stopped in the street and prayed together. But here it's really hard. People think I'm weird because I leave class or miss a bit of break.

Muslim teachings:
- 'Keep up prayer at both ends of the day and at the approach of night. Good deeds remove evil deeds.' (Qur'an 96:19)
- Prayer is very important in Islam, but prayer must be from the heart to be effective.

Dilemma 2

I am quite happy with my looks but I do wish I had a smaller nose, like this girl in my class who all the boys fancy. Can I have cosmetic surgery to fix it?

Muslim teachings:
- The Qur'an says that Satan (the devil) commands people 'to change what Allah has created'. (Qur'an 4:119)
- In his Hadith, Muhammad is said to have cursed 'the tattooer and the person who is tattooed and the one who shortens the teeth and one whose teeth are shortened'.
- The general rule in Islam is that you should be satisfied with the way God has created you. Muslims say the following prayer whenever they look into a mirror, 'O Lord, you have made me beautiful so make my character beautiful too'.

Dilemma 3

I am a Muslim girl and I really enjoy online chatting. I've made loads of friends this way, both girls and boys. Is it allowed for me to chat with boys? I don't talk to anyone who uses bad language or who is disrespectful but sometimes boys do ask for my picture. Is it OK to send it to them if they are Muslim?

Muslim teachings:
- 'Say to believing women to turn their eyes away [from temptation] and preserve their sexual purity.' (Qur'an 24:31)
- 'O mankind! We created you from a single male and female, and made you into nations and tribes, that you may know each other.' (Qur'an 49:13)
- Muhammad once said to his disciples, 'Never look at a woman a second time'.
- Muhammad said, 'Whenever a man and a woman are alone the third one is the devil.'

Dilemma 4

I am a Muslim boy and have a great bunch of mates, both Muslim and non-Muslim. But now all that looks like it's over. I'm sorry to say it, but there's a girl at school who acts in a really bad way. She treated one of my mates really badly. We saw her in town yesterday and all my mates shouted at her, the worst words they knew. I didn't join in because it is so wrong to do this, but my mates say I should've joined in or it's like I think what she did was OK. So I sent her a really bad text. Now I feel bad.

Muslim teachings:
- 'Say to believing men to lower their gazes and restrain their desires.' (Qur'an 24:30)
- Muhammad said, 'When you see evil stop it if you can, otherwise speak out against it and the least you can do is to hate it.'
- Muhammad said, 'The worst people are those who gossip and backbite to create rifts among friends.'
- Muhammad said, 'A Muslim is one from whose hand and tongue other people are safe.'

Dilemma 5

My friends smoke and drink and nothing bad happens to them. Why shouldn't I?

Muslim teachings:
- 'The drinking of alcohol and gambling… are filthy habits of the devil – avoid them.' (Qur'an 5:90)
- 'They ask thee concerning wine and gambling. Say "In them is great sin".' (Qur'an 2:219)
- 'O ye who believe! Approach not prayers with a mind befogged, until ye can understand all that ye say…' (Qur'an 4:43)
- Many Muslim imams today teach that smoking is offensive and undesirable.

Dilemma 6

I'm really ashamed of my Muslim girl friends. I am the only one who covers my face in public, even though this is as God wills. They are no better than all the non-Muslim girls who walk around almost naked. I tell them where they are going wrong to help them, but they say wearing a veil isn't what makes you a good Muslim. What do they mean?

Muslim teachings:
- Covering the face (niqab) is a custom in some Muslim countries, but it is not required by the Qur'an or recommended in Muhammad's teachings.
- The Qur'an does say that Muslim women should cover their whole body, apart from the face, hands and feet.
- Muhammad said, 'A Muslim is one from whose hand and tongue other people are safe.'

Knowing what's right and wrong

objective

to be able to describe some principles in Islam about right and wrong, to interpret teachings on moral values, and to express your ideas on these issues

glossary

Makkah

Most people like to be around other people – at least some of the time! Human beings like to live together as families and work and play with different people. But being around other people is not always easy, because we have to share, care, be kind and overlook people's mistakes. Living alongside other people can be complicated too – there are all sorts of rules about what you should and shouldn't do.

Islam teaches some principles to help people to live together and to know right from wrong. These are called moral values. Other religions also respect and teach these moral values. Some of them are shown in diagram A.

> **1 a** If you were to give someone *one* piece of advice on how to get on with people in your school, what would it be? Explain why it is so important.
>
> **b** Now compare your pieces of advice with the rest of the class. Did you all think the same?

A Eight moral values.

Muhammad said, 'The best amongst you is the person with the best moral virtues.' Once someone asked him, 'What works would take me to paradise?' Muhammad replied, 'Be aware of Allah and be morally good.'

Diseases of the heart

B Islam teaches that people should be patient and not give way to anger.

Muslims believe that there are particular habits or ways of behaving which spoil our relationships. These are known as diseases of the heart. Eight of these 'diseases' are: anger, lying, jealousy, selfishness, boasting, arrogance, hatred, and vanity.

C

Anger	Truthfulness
Lying	Justice
Jealousy	Honesty
Selfishness	Forgiveness
Boasting	Humility
Arrogance	Patience
Hatred	Kindness
Vanity	Generosity

2 Find the opposites to the eight diseases of the heart from the list of good moral values in **C**.

Patience

When things go wrong, Muslims are taught to

'seek Allah's help with patient perseverance and prayer. Allah is with those that are patient.'

(Qur'an 2:153)

Muhammad said, 'When a person falls ill, becomes worried, grief stricken or even if a thorn pricks him, Allah forgives him. Allah forgives his sins.' This teaches that Muslims should be patient in difficult times and remember that they will earn rewards from God for their sufferings.

3 What do you think Muhammad's teaching means? Why would God forgive the sins of those who are suffering?

Generosity

D

Once the Prophet told a story of a generous farmer. He said: 'A man was walking on a moor when he suddenly heard a voice calling to a cloud, "Go and water the orchard of so and so." The man was surprised as he saw the cloud drifting towards an orchard. Then it rained on it. The man followed the cloud over to the orchard. He saw a farmer busy working with a spade. He went up to him and asked his name: it was the same name he had heard before. He was very puzzled. He asked the farmer what was special about him that clouds came especially to water his orchard. The farmer said, "I estimate what the orchard will produce and then I give one third to charity, another third I spend on my family and I invest one third back into the orchard."'

4 a Read story **D**. Why do you think that the cloud came especially to water the farmer's orchard?

b Do you think the farmer was right to only spend a third of what he earned on his family?

c If our government acted like the farmer, do you think poverty in Africa would end? What would life be like for us in this country?

Kindness

One of the greatest goals in Islam is to show kindness to all living creatures. God is often called 'Rahman' in the Qur'an, which means 'the most kind'. Muhammad taught 'be kind to people on earth so that the one in heaven will be kind to you.'

A Muslim army led by Muhammad conquered the city of **Makkah**. On the road, Muhammad saw a dog that had just given birth to a litter of puppies. She was scared by the soldiers and was growling. Muhammad told one of his disciples to stand next to the dog to make sure no one harmed her or her puppies.

5 Patience, generosity and kindness are all very important moral values in Islam. Imagine the government is running three TV adverts to make people more patient, more generous and kinder in everyday life. The government has asked you to come up with some ideas for each advert. Create a spider diagram showing your ideas.

Family life

objective

to be able to explain the roles of parents and children in Muslim families, to describe the reasons behind arranged marriages and to be able to express your own views on love, marriage and family

glossary

Mahr
Sunnah

Muslims believe the family is at the centre of a good society. Everything else is built on it. Islam also recognises that good families don't just *happen*. Everyone in a family has to work at making it good – a family is a team effort.

A What prizes would you award in your family – or a TV family like from a soap or the Simpsons?

Relationships with parents

Muslims believe that parents are to be obeyed and listened to carefully. When parents reach old age, their children should take care of them. In this country, as over the world, Muslims usually ask their parents to come and live with them when they get old. The Qur'an says:

'…Show kindness to your parents. If either or both of them reach old age in your dwelling, show them no sign of impatience, nor rebuke them; but speak to them kind words. Treat them with humility and tenderness and say, "Lord be merciful to them. They nursed me when I was an infant."'

(Qur'an 17:23)

1 Why do you think old people's homes are very rare in Muslim countries? Use the Qur'an quote about showing kindness to parents in your answer.

Relationships with children

Muslim parents see their children as a gift from God, to be loved and cared for and brought up in the Muslim faith. Parents should treat all their children equally and with fair discipline. Muhammad said about his daughter, Fatimah:

'She is my flesh and blood. Anything that worries her will worry me, and anything that hurts her will hurt me.'

(Hadith)

Mothers

The mother is at the heart of the Muslim family. Mothers have the most important responsibility of holding a family together and supporting it in every way. In Islam, mothers are in charge of the home and what they say, goes!

Women in a Muslim family are also responsible for teaching children about Islam and bringing them up in the Muslim faith. When children are very young, they might learn stories about Muhammad's life and from the Qur'an. By the time they are seven, children should have started to learn about prayer and fasting.

Fathers

In a Muslim family, fathers are expected to support their families. This means it is the responsibility of the men in a family to go out to work. Women can go out to work too, but the main responsibility of women in a family is to look after children and older relatives.

The father is the leader of the family because he is responsible for providing for the family and protecting it. Like the mother is responsible for how the family works inside the home, the father must look after the family in the world outside. This means family members should obey what the father says – as long as this doesn't go against what Islam teaches.

Marriage

Muslims believe that the only right way for a man and a woman to live together is as a married couple. Muhammad said, 'Marriage is my **Sunnah** [my way] and whoever doesn't practise this is not from my followers.'

Because marriage is so important, Muslim parents often take on the responsibility of arranging the marriage of their children. However, parents cannot force their children to marry someone against their will.

Three things have to happen for a marriage ceremony to take place:
1 The bride and groom must give their permission.
2 There must be two Muslim witnesses.
3 The groom must give a substantial gift to the bride, called **mahr**. This is to show his commitment to the marriage and his respect for the bride's family.

Ⓑ

2 What are the team responsibilities in your family?

3 Many men and women in the West today put everything they have into their careers. What do you think a Muslim would say about this?

4 Explain why many Muslim parents arrange their children's marriages.

The Qur'an says:

'Among His signs is that Allah created for you spouses [husband and wife] from among yourselves so that you may live in peace, and planted love and kindness in your hearts.'

(Qur'an 30:21)

5 This verse says that love between people is a sign of God's existence. How do you explain the existence of love in the world?

Sawm

What is sawm?

Sawm is the fourth pillar of Islam (pages 8–9) and is fasting during the Islamic month of **Ramadan**. Muhammad received the first revelation from God during Ramadan, so this is a special time for Muslims everywhere.

Sawm is about using your own strength of mind to gain control over your body. During Ramadan, Muslim adults do not eat or drink from dawn to dusk. During each day, they avoid anything bad, like quarrelling, swearing, cheating or lying. They give more time to worshipping God. This includes additional prayers, going to the **mosque** more frequently and reading the whole Qur'an.

A After the sun sets, the fast is broken with a meal known as iftar.

At the end of Ramadan is a festival to celebrate successfully completing the fast. This celebration is known as **Eid-ul-Fitr**.

Activity

1 a Make a list of all the things you've eaten or drunk so far today.

   b Now imagine you are taking part in a sponsored one-day fast for charity. Write a diary entry for your day, describing how you feel and what you miss most.

2 The Hadith teaches that not lying to people is more important in sawm than not eating or drinking. Why do you think this is?

objective

to be able to explain sawm as a way of taking responsibility for actions and consider what fasting would be like and relate what you know to why some Muslims say fasting is important to them

glossary

Eid-ul-Fitr
Mosque
Ramadan
Sawm

Why do Muslims fast?

Going without food or drink every day for a month is very hard. It would be very easy to cheat – to have a sip of water or a quick snack when no one was around. But Muslims believe God is always watching, so cheating in this way would only be cheating yourself. Islam is about submitting to the will of God, and sawm tests and teaches this obedience. It is part of each Muslim's personal responsibility towards God. The Qur'an says:

'O believers, fasting is obligatory for you so that you can become god-fearing and pious.'

(Qur'an 2:183)

B

What Muhammad taught about fasting:
- 'Fasting is a shield against attacks by the devil.'
- 'The reward for fasting is forgiveness of previous sins.'
- 'There is a special gate in Heaven reserved for the fasting people.'

There are lots of reasons why sawm is so important. In 2005, a survey asked UK Muslims what Ramadan meant to them. Here are some of the answers people sent in.

C What does sawm mean to you?

> For me, Ramadan is wonderful because it brings all Muslims together and shows the world what Islam is really about.

> At Ramadan I can feel for myself the hunger and thirst of the poor. I feel connected with them and can thank God for all he has given me.

> My non-Muslim friends say they feel sorry for me but I think Ramadan is a great experience. It brings friends and family together. You realise how much we have to be thankful for.

> Ramadan is when I reflect on my life and all the things my faith brings me. Ramadan brings me closer to God.

> Ramadan is not just about fasting; it's about stopping ourselves from doing all the things Allah tells us not to do. Once you have tried to do this for the month of Ramadan, you reconnect with how God wishes you to live your life all the year through.

> We are surrounded by so much stress in our lives, so much rushing around and trying to sort things out. Then Ramadan comes and all that stress and panic dies down; you realise again what is important in life. Ramadan teaches me each year who I am and what life is for.

Activity

3 a Look through the quotes from the survey. List the different reasons people give for why sawm is important to them. How many match what Muhammad taught about fasting in **B**?

b Now divide up your list in *three* ways: reasons that are to do with personal responsibility; reasons that involve being part of the Muslim community; and reasons to do with responsibility to poor people.

4 Sometimes non-Muslims fast during Ramadan to help their Muslim friends. Do you think this is a good idea? Explain your reasons.

Mosques and the community

objective

to show your understanding of the role of mosques in Muslim communities and be able to explain how Muslims in the UK have faced prejudice

glossary

Islamiat
Madrasah
Terrorism

Muhammad established a mosque at his house. Here, people came to pray, learn, find shelter, rest and make decisions. Mosques today still do the same things. A mosque is not only a place to pray, it is a real community centre. This is especially true in countries like the UK, where the majority of people are not Muslims.

Mosques have lots of different functions for their local community. Diagram **A** shows some of them.

The local mosque is not just important for adults: it is a big part of the lives of children too. Many British Muslim teenagers go to a **madrasah** each day after they have finished school. A madrasah teaches Islamic studies – called **Islamiat**. It is often part of a mosque, or in a building somewhere else but run by a local mosque. Most Muslim children in a community study their religion together at their madrasah, so it is an important way of holding a community together and keeping important traditions going. It is a big time commitment for young people.

A

- Place for prayer
- Place for celebrations, e.g. marriages
- Funeral services
- Sports and social: games/community room, used for parties, etc.
- **Mosque**
- Further learning: place for lectures, reading room, bookshop, etc.
- Law court. decisions made here (Islamic law)
- Education: the madrasah (Islamic school)

B

I go to madrasah every school night for about an hour and a half. We learn passages from the Holy Qur'an, Arabic, about Muslim history and the life of the Prophet. We learn how to pray the five daily prayers and about the duties of a Muslim and how to live a good life. There are loads of tests but it's OK because you get certificates and even trophies when you pass them. I like learning Arabic but it is hard, especially when you're tired after a day at school.

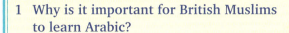
C A madrasah

1 Why is it important for British Muslims to learn Arabic?

2 Put together your own 10-question test on Islam, and design a certificate for those people who pass it. When designing, remember that having pictures of people or living things is un-Islamic.

3 Explain how you think a Muslim teenager in this country might feel about finishing school, having a quick tea and then going to madrasah for more lessons every school night.

What makes a community?

Muslims all feel part of one global community of Islam. In the UK, a mosque might serve a community made up of just a few Muslim families, or many hundreds. Those families might have roots in many countries around the world, or everyone might have family roots in the same country or region.

Many young British Muslims have parents and grandparents who came to the UK 30 or 40 years ago. Many came from Pakistan and Bangladesh. At that time, they faced a lot of racism from white British people. Muslim families built up communities together but, because of the racism, could not always make strong links with the white communities around them. Mosques were very important for making people feel connected with their own culture, religion, and their community.

Today, although young British Muslims have grown up in UK culture, the community their parents built is still a strong part of their lives. Being a Muslim is something that's very important to people, whether it is a faith people have grown up in, or a choice people make later in life. Unfortunately, British Muslims still face a lot of prejudice. **Terrorist** attacks in New York in 2001 and in London in 2005 have fuelled this – along with a lot of ignorance about Islam. Muslim communities today have many strong links with the other communities around them. However, there is still much to be done to stop prejudice against Muslim communities in this country.

4 What links do you have with your local community? Display them in a spider diagram.

5 Some Muslims who settled in this country decided that no matter what horrible things white people said to them, they would just keep on treating them with respect until the white people finally returned their respect. Do you think this was right? How would you act to combat prejudice?

6 Prejudice is usually based on ignorance and stupidity. What could local mosques do to educate the wider community about Islam and their community?

D Should these British Muslims dress differently to avoid prejudice?

Muslim Youth Helpline

objective

to be able to describe how the MYH is helping young people in the Muslim community and explain why the organisation was set up and to express your own views on the responsibilities of others

glossary

Tawhid

The Muslim Youth Helpline (MYH) is a confidential helpline for young people living in the UK. It was set up by young people to respond to the problems young Muslims face in Britain today.

Since it was set up in 2001, the MYH has dealt with over 7,000 enquiries. The top problems raised by callers are: family, relationships, sexuality, drugs, and mental health problems like depression.

The majority of the people who work for MYH are between 18 and 25 years of age. The idea is that young people will find it easier to talk to other young people. The MYH founders believe that the older generations in Muslim communities do not always understand their children's problems. All MYH workers are Muslims and receive basic training in counselling skills. MYH counselling is based around Islamic values, which means that Helpline workers are trained to be non-judgmental, tolerant and open to listening to others without making them feel like they are doing something wrong.

Helpline workers are all volunteers. They all complete an intensive 60-hour training course in counselling skills, telephone, e-mail skills and case studies. Helpline workers need really good 'people skills' and should be:

- sympathetic
- supportive
- respectful of someone's right to make their own decisions
- non-judgmental.

1 Do you agree that young people are more likely to talk to other young people about problems?

The MYH has developed a course for all Helpline workers that includes an introduction to Islamic counselling. The role of the Helpline worker is to listen to the person regardless of religious belief or practice, and to explore practical ways of moving forward. Although Helpline workers are all Muslims, religious opinions are only given if the caller or e-mailer specifically asks for them – and are not given by the Helpline worker. These religious opinions are always passed on to a Muslim scholar for answering.

Faridha Karim of MYH explains that:

Islamic counselling is based on Islamic etiquette and values and relates basic Islamic principles such as the Oneness of God (**Tawhid**) to the way you relate to others as a counsellor. It means being non-judgemental, tolerant and open to listening to people's problems without making value judgements, condemning or chastising. It means remembering that human beings are created with flaws and weaknesses and that we should support one another in overcoming them. Other than that, it's not necessarily a different form of counselling to others – it's just keeping those principles in mind in the approach.

C

Case study

Laila is 18 years old and her family comes from Pakistan. She says that she's really stuck as to what to do since her mother doesn't want her to go to university, because she may be getting married soon when the family goes to Pakistan this summer. She doesn't think she'll be getting married for definite, because her brother is one year older.

Laila spoke to a female counsellor who explored what options were available to her. She decided that she didn't mind getting married soon, but she wanted to carry on with her education and become an architect. The counsellor encouraged her to speak with her mother and reach a compromise. She now hopes to attend a local college.

2 a What responsibilities would a volunteer for the MYH be taking on?

  b How stressful do you think the job would be?

3 Why might a young Muslim volunteer to work on the MYH? List at least *three* reasons.

4 If MYH workers are all Muslims, why do you think they are not allowed to give religious opinions when people ask for them?

5 Does Laila's story support the MYH's argument that Muslim young people need a special Muslim helpline service? Explain your answer.

Shareefa Fulat, who works for the MYH, explains that young Muslims are often confused about where they fit in to British society. She says:

D E-mail to MYH, 2004

To: help@myh.org.uk

Cc:

Attachments:

Thank you to the people who I have now declared my guardian angels… Thank you for your kind words and advice. Your warm e-mails were the only thing that kept me going for a while and though it all happened so quickly, your e-mailers have touched me in an outstanding way that will stay with me forever.

What exacerbates these problems is that there are no support services, or support from within the Muslim community, for people struggling with resolving their identities. There are huge cultural and generational differences within the community which also play a role.

6 Design a leaflet to promote the MYH, using the information on these two pages to help you. Your leaflet should:

- reassure young people that the MYH is confidential

- explain that the MYH provides Islamic counselling

- show how the MYH can help young people deal with their problems.

Social responsibilities

objective

to be able to explain what you think makes a good citizen and to describe how well someone's actions fit with Islam's teachings on people's responsibilities to others

Islam teaches that human beings are all 'Allah's family'. We are all brothers and sisters to one another and we are all equal. Muslims believe God wishes people to be good to each other, to respect one another and to look after each other. Muhammad taught:

'Every one of you is like a shepherd and is responsible for his flock. The ruler is a shepherd, so is the husband who is responsible for his family. The wife is a shepherd too who looks after the household and children. So every one of you is a shepherd and every one of you is responsible for his flock.'

(Hadith)

A How does the shepherd show care for his flock?

Muslims believe they have two kinds of responsibilities:
1 Responsibilities to God – this means believing in God, worshipping and obeying him.
2 Responsibilities to fellow humans – this means caring for others. We call these social responsibilities.

Muhammad taught that Muslims must think of others as well as themselves and their close family. Once he said, 'You cannot be a believer until you are kind to your neighbour.'

One day, Muhammad smelt the soup his wife was cooking. He told her to give some of it to the neighbours who could also smell it. He said that it was not right for a Muslim to sleep with a full stomach after having had a good meal while his neighbours were hungry.

What makes a good citizen?

We are all members of lots of different groups: a group of friends, a group of people who go to the same school, a local community, a part of the country, a country, etc. A good citizen is usually thought of as someone who lives up to their responsibilities for others. All communities have rules to help them run smoothly. A good citizen keeps to those rules. All communities need people to work for others as well as for themselves. A good citizen gets involved in making a community work for everyone.

A Activity

1 a **Read the different statements in B. Which ones do you think describe a good citizen? List your choices.**

b **Which of these would be your top *three* qualities a good citizen should have? Add your own descriptions if you need to.**

B

> Collects money for a local charity.

> Watches out of window for young people looking suspicious.

> Prays regularly.

> Recycles newspapers and bottles.

> Reports noisy neighbours.

> Votes in elections.

> Keeps to the speed limit.

> Asks people to pick up litter they've dropped.

> Protests against a local factory that causes harmful pollution.

> Helps out at local old people's home.

Zahid Malik – a good citizen?

Zahid Malik is a police officer with Nottinghamshire Police Force. Read what he says about his life and then carry out the activities that follow.

C

'Both my parents were born in Mirpur, Pakistan. My father arrived in England in the mid 1950s. I was born in Nottingham. As a child, I have many happy memories of my parents doing their utmost to provide and look after my family...

In October 1985, at the age of 20, I joined Nottinghamshire Police Force and was the first British Pakistani officer. I immersed myself in my work and worked hard. After some nine years I received Divisional Commendations for good work.

Between 1996 and 2003, I worked as a Beat Manager in Keyworth Village. This was a more community-focused job and I enjoyed working and policing this small community. I spent many years working closely with the local schools and community organisations as well as working very closely with the local Parish Council. In 1999, I... was awarded The Christopher McDonald Trophy for "Nottinghamshire Police Community Constable of the Year 1999–2000".

I have... recently been involved with promoting Islam awareness to selected groups within Nottinghamshire's Police Force. I am married and have four children. My eldest daughter is currently at university studying for her English degree. My 15-year-old son currently attends the Nottingham Islamia School. I feel blessed to be born into a Muslim family and have always endeavoured to positively portray myself as a police officer who is a Muslim.'

Activity

2 a **List the different ways in which Zahid helps his community.**

b **Zahid was the first British Pakistani officer to join Nottinghamshire Police Force. Why do you think he might have chosen this career? What problems might he have faced in his first years with the Police?**

c **Zahid worked closely with the community in Keyworth Village and won an award for his work. How can the Police help a community run properly? Make a list of at least *five* things in your answer.**

d **What do you think 'promoting Islam awareness' involves? Put together a recruitment poster to encourage more British Muslims to become community police officers.**

British Muslims?

Islam teaches that people should try their best to become good citizens. Muslims should honour the laws where they live – as long as these laws do not go against the teachings of Islam.

As well as obeying the law, Islam urges Muslims to treat other people well. In following God's will, Muslims should be:

- kind
- helpful
- fair to all
- peaceful and respectful.

Activity

1 a How do you think a good citizen should behave? Compare your list with the values Islam teaches.

b What makes you proud to be living in this country? What don't you like about this country?

c Draw a spider diagram to show what British citizenship means to you.

Muslims in the UK

There are around 1.6 million Muslims living in the UK: that's 3% of the population. A third of these are under 16 years old. Although almost all young Muslims in Britain were born here, many find living in the UK difficult. Life got much harder for UK Muslims after the terrorist attacks in New York in 2001 and London in 2005. Although Muslim communities across the UK condemned the attacks, lots of people blamed all Muslims for what had happened.

A These British Muslims are protesting against the July '05 attacks in London.

A BBC Newsround survey after 11 September 2001 found that:

- four out of ten Muslim children in the survey thought the news always portrayed Muslims in a bad light
- one in three Muslim children said they'd been bullied; half of those were bullied because of their religion
- seven out of ten Muslim children thought of themselves as Muslim rather than British.

Another survey in the *Muslim News* (2005) asked Muslims in the UK what they felt about their identity. Many people replied, with various views. A few of them are shown in **B**.

 B

A I am a practising Muslim and a loyal British citizen. If the State starts interfering with my religious obligations I will struggle, within the Law, to change things. If unsuccessful I will migrate.

B If eating fish and chips, wearing a pinstripe suit makes me British so be it, as this is OK with Islam, but if supporting British troops in Iraq makes me British then I am definitely not that.

C If someone asks me what religion I am, I say – Muslim and proud, but if someone asks what nationality am I, I say – British, because that's where I was born, but I am first a Muslim, and British after.

D I do not feel British at all. I have been, and am still, experiencing, racial, ethnic, national and religious discrimination since I came here 10 years ago.

E What seems to be coming out here is that we should take on British values just because we live here as they have a long tradition. What are these values? Why should we adopt them? What happens if another set of values is based on a stronger rationale?

F I would label myself as a Muslim because religion is the first part to my identity and no one can change that because that's who I am. I don't believe in terrorism and I respect others and luv every1 around me and am still a good Muslim and I fink dats da strongest fing of all.

G Nationality shouldn't be important. Way of Life [i.e. Islam] should be.

A Hadith says:

'On the day of judgement Allah will say, "Where are those who befriended and loved one another for the sake of my Glory? Today I shall shelter them in my shade when there is no other shade."'

(Hadith)

Activity

2 Read through the speech bubbles in **B**. Which quote(s):

   a match the Islamic teaching on citizenship at the start of this topic

   b say that Islam is more important than nationality

   c question why Muslims should become British first and Muslim second?

3 Many young Muslims feel they live good lives and treat other people well and, yet, some non-Muslims still disrespect them. People clearly need to know more about Islam. Plan a government advertising campaign to encourage people to find out more about Islam.

Assessment for Unit 2

> O people, listen to my words carefully, for I do not know whether I will meet you again on such an occasion as this.
>
> You must live at peace with one another. Everyone must respect the rights and properties of their neighbours. There must be no rivalry or enmity among you. Just as you regard this month as sacred, so regard the life and property of every Muslim in the same way. Remember, you will surely appear before God and answer for your actions.
>
> All believers are brothers… you are not allowed to take things from another Muslim unless he gives it to you willingly. You are to look after your families with all your heart, and be kind to the women God has entrusted to you.
>
> You have been left God's Book, the Qur'an. If you hold fast to it, and do not let it go, you will not stray from the right path. People, reflect on my words… I leave behind me two things, the Qur'an and the example of my life. If you follow these you will not fail.
>
> Listen to me very carefully. Worship God, be steadfast in prayer, fast during Ramadan, pay alms to the less fortunate…
>
> (Muhammad's Last Sermon; Hadith)

These questions test different sets of skills in RE. Which skills do you need to work on? Choose the level you need and work through the tasks set.

Level 3

- Read the passage here from Muhammad's last sermon. Write down *three* things Muhammad says in this sermon which tell Muslims how to look after other people.
- What might Muslims say if you asked them what they thought of having to give money (zakah) each year?
- Why do people spend more money on family and friends at Christmas time than at any other times of the year?

Level 4

- Muhammad said, 'I leave behind me two things, the Qur'an and the example of my life.' Give *three* examples from your reading of ways in which Muhammad's life shows people how to behave.
- Explain why it is important for Muslims to have a religious marriage ceremony rather than a civil one. Describe the impact believing in Islam has on responsibilities in a Muslim family.
- Describe an occasion when you chose to do something for someone else and got nothing out of it. What made you do it?

Level 5

- Explain why Muslims believe they should take responsibility for the welfare of people they may never have met.
- Describe the connection between sawm (fasting during Ramadan) and the responsibilities to the less fortunate Muhammad spoke of in his last sermon.
- Why do you think Muslims get involved in fighting humam rights abuse? Do you consider it matters very much if it happens in a far away country or even if it happens here? Explain your reasons.

Level 6

- Islam has a strong focus on justice and equality, yet some in the West criticise the practice in many Muslim cultures of treating men and women differently. Muhammad's last sermon was nearly 1400 years ago. When he told Muslim men to 'be kind to the women God has entrusted to you', do you think this was promoting the equality of women and men, or not? Give reasons for your view.
- Compare the way a Muslim makes decisions about right and wrong actions, with the way a non-religious person decides. What sorts of things guide your decisions about right and wrong actions?
- Muhammad's last sermon emphasises that all believers should live in peace together. Jesus also told his followers to 'love your neighbour as you love yourself'. Do religions help communities get along together, or not? Explain your views.

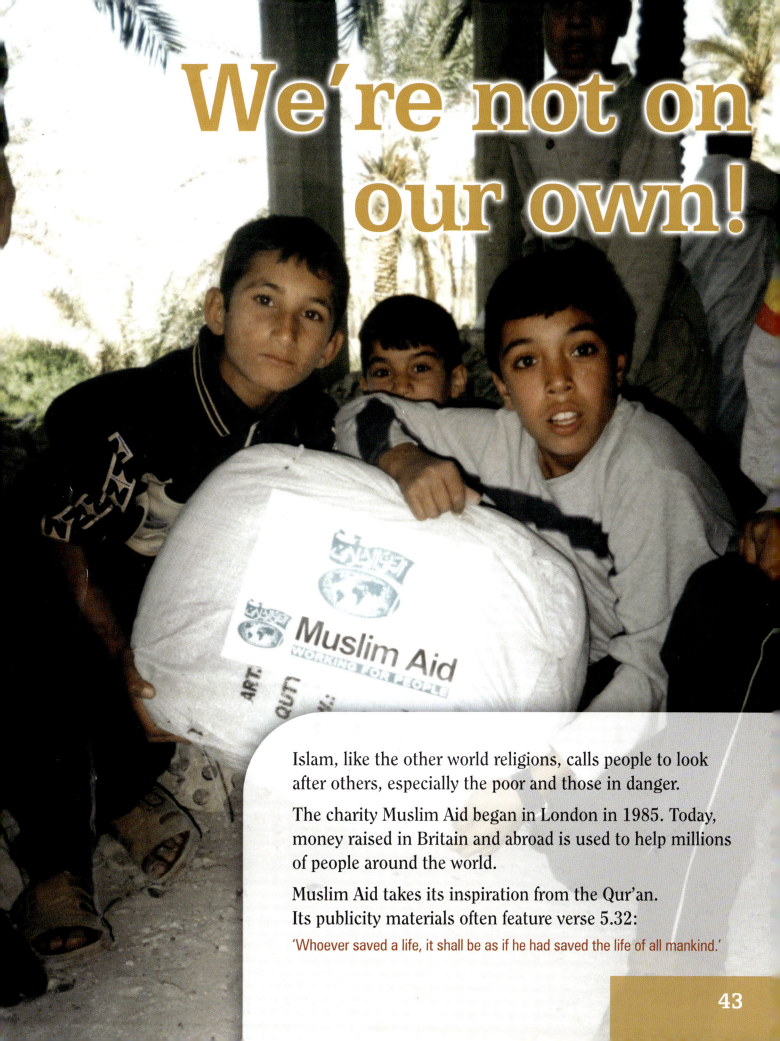

We're not on our own!

Islam, like the other world religions, calls people to look after others, especially the poor and those in danger.

The charity Muslim Aid began in London in 1985. Today, money raised in Britain and abroad is used to help millions of people around the world.

Muslim Aid takes its inspiration from the Qur'an. Its publicity materials often feature verse 5.32:

'Whoever saved a life, it shall be as if he had saved the life of all mankind.'

Rich and poor

objective

to be able to explain Islam's teachings on poverty and show your understanding of three particularly teachings on poverty

glossary

Qur'an

A How do the needs of poor people in Britain compare with the needs of poor people in countries like Mali, Africa?

What is poverty?

There are poor people all over the world; people who don't have the money to lead a comfortable life. This state of being poor is called poverty.

Islam teaches that poor and needy people must be cared for by people who are better-off. God promises to reward those who spend their wealth on the poor. The **Qur'an** says about rich people:

'And in their wealth is the share of the beggars and deprived.'

(Qur'an 70:25)

This is a key teaching on poverty. The language is quite complicated, so what does it mean exactly? We could rephrase it like this:

beggars and deprived people are owed a share of the wealth of well-off people.

So Islam teaches that the poor have a right to a share in the wealth of the rich. This makes it clear that when the rich give to the poor, they are not doing them a favour but fulfilling their own responsibility. They are spending in God's way.

Remember that Islam is about following God's will. Since people's wealth is given to them by God in the first place, he expects them to share it with others. Spending in God's ways is highly praised (**B**).

B The Qur'an says:

'Those who spend their wealth in Allah's way is like a grain of corn which brings forth seven ears, each bearing a hundred grains. Allah gives plenty to whom he pleases. He is generous and knowing.'

[Qur'an 2:261]

Activity

1 Do you think the poor have a right to the wealth of the rich? What might some rich people say against this?

2 a Study the parable of the corn in **B**. What does the word 'parable' mean?

 b Explain this parable in your own words.

Sharing

Sharing what you have with others stops people from becoming greedy. Greed stops people from building lasting relationships with other people. It makes people selfish and we tend not to trust selfish people. In Islam, greed is regarded as an evil that leads to sufferings, like wars and pollution. In the following quote from the Qur'an, God praises people who give up what they have to help others.

'They love those who have sought refuge with them, they entertain no desire in their hearts for what they are given… Those who can stop being greedy are really successful.'

(Qur'an 59:9)

3 Muslims believe greed leads to bad things like pollution and war. What sorts of greed could lead to a war? List your thoughts and compare them with others in your group.

How Muhammad praised spending on the poor

Islam aims to help people become better human beings by constantly encouraging and spurring them on to be selfless and kind. For Muslims, Muhammad is the best role-model for people to follow. Muhammad was always generous to the needy.

4 Read each of the three stories about Muhammad in **C** carefully to reveal their meanings.

a Did you find Story 3 the easiest to understand? This story uses lively words and phrases to build a strong picture of Muhammad and his teachings in our minds. What point is it making? List the words that make the story lively and interesting.

b Did you find Story 1 the hardest to understand? Use the following tips to reveal its meaning:

> you = the disciples/people generally
>
> spending in the way of Allah = spend money as God wishes it
>
> because of spending = if you spend

c Story 1 sets out a contradiction. What teaching on these pages explains why people could become richer by giving more of their money away?

d What did Muhammad mean when he put two of his fingers together in Story 2? Using metaphors or similes are very powerful ways of helping people understand something complex. What other metaphors or similes could you use to explain that one thing is very close to something else?

e Story 2 explains that those who care for orphans will be close to Muhammad in paradise. There are lots of ways to help those in need. Why would caring for orphans be singled out in this way?

C

1 Once Muhammad said to his disciples, 'You will not become poor because of spending in the way of Allah.'

2 The Prophet praised those who cared for orphans; he said, 'I and the person who looks after an orphan will enter paradise together like this,' then he raised his forefinger and middle finger together.

3 One day the Prophet prayed with the congregation. As soon as he finished, he jumped up and rushed off. Everyone was surprised at his haste. When he returned he said, 'I remembered that I had left a gold coin in my room and I wanted to make sure I spent it in Allah's way before the nightfall.'

Zakah

objective

to be able to describe how zakah works to help the poor and explain the things zakah can be used for; to give your own evaluation of zakah

glossary

Mosque
Sadaqah
Zakah

The third pillar of Islam is called **zakah** – which is like charity. Zakah is compulsory. Every Muslim who is able to provide for his or her family's needs must pay 2.5% from their annual savings to help those in need.

Muslims believe that whatever they own really belongs to God and must be spent as God would want. This includes sharing some of what they have with those in need. Zakah means a community isn't completely split into the 'haves' and 'have nots'.

Muhammad said,

'You cannot be a true believer until you wish for your brother what you wish for yourself.'

(Hadith)

The word 'zakah' means 'to cleanse' or 'to purify'. Muslims believe that zakah cleans out the love of money and greediness from people. God does not wish money to be used selfishly. The wealth that God gives to people should be used to help people live as God wishes.

A The Qur'an states that Muslims who give zakah will be rewarded with heaven.

1 a Explain what a Muslim means by zakah.

b Islam teaches that all wealth is God's and should be spent in a way in which God would approve. What sort of things would not be right for Muslims to spend money on?

c The Qur'an encourages people to give zakah privately rather than in a big, showy way. Why do you think this is?

What is zakah used for?

The Qur'an says:

'Alms are for the poor and the needy, and those employed to administer the [funds]; for those whose hearts have been [recently] reconciled [to the truth]; for those in bondage and in debt; in the cause of Allah; and for the wayfarer: [thus is it] ordained by Allah, and Allah is full of knowledge and wisdom.'

(Qur'an 9:60)

2 Read the passage from the Qur'an above, which lists the people who should be given the money from zakah. Match the types of people in **B** with their definitions.

People

The poor.	The needy.
The administrators of zakah.	Recent converts to Islam.
Those in bondage.	Those who are in debt.
For the cause of God.	Those who are stranded during a journey.

Definition

Travellers having difficulties on their journeys because of loss of money or breakdown of vehicles which they don't have money to repair, etc.	People who are thinking about becoming Muslims or have already converted to Islam.
People with no way of making a living, no possessions.	People who don't have enough, nor have the basic necessities, to support their families.
Used to pay off the debts of a person who has borrowed money to pay for basic necessities so that he or she can lead a normal life.	People who collect and organise the zakah money.
Used to free slaves or captives.	People who support any kind of work or struggle in God's name.

Sadaqah

As well as compulsory zakah, Muslims who want to contribute more to helping others can give **sadaqah**. This is a voluntary act of charity given to thank God. For example, Muslims may give money to celebrate a wedding, help good causes, contribute to building a new **mosque** or a new school or hospital, or to help victims of war or disaster. Many Muslims sponsor orphans around the world as well as meeting their zakah commitments.

Is zakah only for the wealthy?

Islam teaches that everyone should give to help others. Muhammad said, 'Zakah is a necessity for every Muslim.'

'But what about someone who is already poor?' someone asked. Muhammad answered, 'He should work with his own hands for his benefit and then give something out of such earnings in zakah.'

Muhammad's companions then asked what would happen if the poor person wasn't able to work. Muhammad replied, 'He should encourage other people to do good.'

When his companions asked what the person should do if he couldn't encourage anyone else to do good deeds, Muhammad said, 'He should stop himself from doing evil. That is also charity.'

3 a Some people would say that 'charity' is not a very complete definition of the word zakah. Having read these teachings by Muhammad on zakah, what do you think? What would be a better definition of zakah?

b Only adults are permitted to give zakah, but what would you think of a similar system that meant you had to donate a fixed amount of your money each year to help others? What would be good about it, and what would you not like about it?

Muslim Hands is one of the largest Muslim charities in the UK. It started in a Nottingham mosque in 1993, during the war in Bosnia. The charity now works in over 30 countries in Africa and Asia. Since its launch, Muslim Hands has been involved in relief work following disasters in Iran, Bangladesh and Pakistan, the Asian tsunami, and wars in Kosovo and Iraq. This topic looks at some of the projects run by Muslim Hands.

A Muslim Hands logo.

Zakah collection

Muslim Hands provides a service for calculating, collecting and spending zakah according to the donors' wishes.

Orphan Sponsorship Scheme

Donors give monthly payments for helping poor families caring for orphans. The sponsorship scheme began in 1994 and is currently running in 22 countries such as Palestine, Pakistan, Iraq, Albania, India and China. The scheme aims to help children in need with food, support, care and, above all, education. The charity sees education as so important because it gives these children a future to look forward to, and increases their chances of supporting themselves in the future. Muslim Hands is currently sponsoring over 5,000 orphans.

Education

Muslim Hands sees education as a right for all, fundamental to the development of prosperous communities, and as the most effective tool for empowering the poor to break out of poverty. The charity offers donors the chance to sponsor a student by paying towards their education.

In 2000, Muslim Hands started a long-term school-building programme designed to raise the standards of education in poor communities. Muslim Hands now has over 120 schools from Kosovo to Kashmir,

Sudan to Sri Lanka. Muslim Hands allows all children to study at the schools but orphans sponsored by the Muslim Hands programme are given priority.

Callers to the Muslim Hands office usually ask: 'What is the best way to spend the money?' and the answer is always 'Sponsor a child today!'

Community schemes

The community schemes are designed to help both individuals and communities by providing essentials such as safe housing and clean water. Donors can help plant trees and fit tube wells in poor communities.

Muslim Hands launches many projects to help the needy in different fields such as education, orphan sponsorship, vocational training, safe water schemes, and many more. Of these, three are largely ongoing where the work is done throughout the year.

Activity

1 The Muslim Hands 'It's My Project' (IMP) scheme has the slogan: 'Your Idea + Muslim Hands skills makes an IMP!'

What project would you suggest for your group's IMP? It could be something small and focused, or a £500,000 major development plan (if you can think of ways to raise the funds you'd need!) Your project should:

- focus on improving education
- be suitable for zakah payments
- fit with Muslim beliefs about helping the poor and needy.

2 The fundraising department of Muslim Hands is always on the move, travelling up and down the country trying to gain as much support as possible. Using the information in this topic, put together a leaflet to encourage people to donate to Muslim Hands projects.

B Little Moon Nursery.

It's My Project (IMP)

IMP gives donors a chance to start their very own project from as little as £250. All projects are done in the name of donors and the donors receive regular feedback on progress.

The Little Moon Nursery in Baghdad, Iraq is an example of a recent IMP. This nursery looked after around 100 children, but was in a very bad state of repair following the 2003 war and the looting that came after it. It cost £6,000 to repair the building and redecorate, to fit air conditioning, and supply learning materials and other essentials like plastic furniture, curtains, a water cooler, carpets and a TV and VCR. The children were also treated to a special party. Since the refurbishment, the nursery now looks after 200 children!

The money for the Little Moon Nursery's repair was raised by people from Bristol Islamic Classes in the UK. Muslim Hands Iraq supervised the work.

Stewards of the earth

objective

to be able to explain Islamic concepts about humans' responsibility to the environment and to compare different views on responsibilities to the environment

glossary

Fitrah
Hadith
Khalifah

Muslims believe that God created all the plants and animals and the beautiful natural world around us. He made the earth as part of the vast solar system with the sun at its centre. Our solar system is a part of a huge universe with billions of stars. Muslims believe that the whole of this universe follows God's laws. These are also called laws of nature: gravity; the climate system; and the cycle of day and night. Everything has a purpose. There is nothing that is useless.

Islam teaches that the earth belongs to God and humans cannot just do what they want with it. The earth is not only for humans but also for all living things. God has given humans a special place in his creation and has put humans in charge of the world as **khalifahs** (stewards or caretakers of the earth). The Qur'an teaches:

'It is He who has made You [His] agents, inheritors of the earth.'   [Qur'an 21:107]

This means that God expects humans to care for the environment. They are responsible for looking after everything on earth. God will hold them accountable for their actions. This teaches Muslims to be extremely careful with nature.

Muslims believe that God created everything in a perfect state. The Qur'an says:

'Therefore set your face in worship to the true faith, the original pure state with which God endowed man. God's creation cannot be changed.'

[Qur'an 30:30]

> **Activity**
>
> 1 a The Qur'an teaches that human beings are khalifahs of the earth. Explain how, as stewards, human beings can care for the world and its resources.
>
> b Are all human beings good khalifahs? List some human actions against the natural world that would not be good stewardship.

A 'It is He who made the sun to be a shining glory.' (Qur'an 10:5)

There is a balance in nature known as **fitrah** that must not be changed. Muslims are taught that they have a duty to care for the natural resources of the planet and all the creatures on it to make sure that this balance is maintained.

Animals

Muslims are taught that they must be good to animals: cruelty to animals is forbidden. Muhammad told many stories about animals to show that following the way of God includes treating animals with kindness and care.

C In one story, Muhammad described how he had found an overworked and underfed camel tied to a post. Muhammad asked its owner, 'Do you not fear Allah because of this camel?' Muhammad explained that God had given the camel into the man's care and he had a duty to treat the camel well. The owner of the camel accepted the teaching and declared, 'I have done wrong.' He accepted that in future he must look after his camels properly and ensure that they had enough food and water.

B Muhammad said, 'Even looking after plants and trees is an act of virtue.' [Hadith]

2 a Read the following **Hadith** of Muhammad and copy it down.

'If a Muslim plants a tree or sows a field and humans and beasts and birds eat from it, all of it is love on his part.'

b Explain what Muhammad was teaching about caring for the environment in this Hadith.

Moderation and balance

Muslims believe that they must not waste anything and only use what is necessary. This means controlling how much of the planet's natural resources we use. The Qur'an says:

'God raised the sky high and set the balance so do not ruin the balance… He spread out the earth for His creation with fruits and blossom bearing palm, grain and scented herbs, which of your Lord's blessings would you deny?'

[Qur'an 55:7–12]

3 Modern environmental science teaches that the environment works as a series of systems, all working together. Environmental problems happen when systems get out of balance.

a How does this theory compare with Muslim views about the environment?

b What would life be like if people all lived in balance with natural systems? Describe the main differences with how we live in the West today.

Putting it into practice

objective

to be able to describe and explain how Muslims respond to animal experimentation and global warming and to compare different views about global warming and ways to combat it

glossary

Ahadith
Dominion
Global warming
Greenhouse effect

Both the Qur'an and **Ahadith** of Muhammad make it clear that Muslims have a duty to care for the environment as they will be judged by God on how they have cared for the world and all that is in it.

Animal rights

Muhammad taught that if Muslims are kind and merciful towards animals, then God will be kind and merciful towards them. Muslims understand this to mean that compassion must be shown to living creatures and plants at all times.

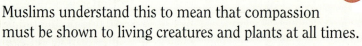

 Do experiments on animals have a just cause?

Muslims believe that all animals are created by God and, although humans have been given **dominion** over them, this does not mean that humans can do what they want with animals. Islam teaches that humans may only take the life of an animal for food or another useful purpose. Even then, every care must be taken to kill the animal with as little pain as possible. A Hadith of Muhammad says:

'Whoever kills anything bigger than a sparrow without a just cause, Allah will hold him accountable for it.'

[Hadith]

1 Experiments on animals are used today for medical research and testing cosmetics. Such practices did not exist at the time of Muhammad, so there is no direct reference to animal experimentation in the Ahadith. From what you've learned about Islamic teachings on animals, how do you think most Muslims would view:

a animal testing to improve cosmetics

b animal testing to improve medical treatments

Global warming

The earth maintains a fine balance with its plants and animals, ensuring that life continues. Plants and animals are very sensitive to the environment. Over the last two centuries, human activities have begun to change the environment in new ways and on a greater scale than ever before.

Huge areas of forest have been cut down and industrialisation has released poisonous chemicals into rivers and oceans.

The vast amounts of coal and oil that we burn release carbon dioxide and other harmful substances into the atmosphere which many scientists believe is causing a **greenhouse effect**. This means that pollutants are sitting in the earth's atmosphere. These act like a blanket, warming the atmosphere and the seas.

There is no doubt that **global warming** is taking place – no one yet knows how much the world will heat up and what the effects will be. Although many believe that humans have created the current rise in the earth's temperature so far, it has not been proved that this is absolutely the case. Nor do scientists or politicians agree on the best way to reduce global warming.

One likely consequence of global warming is a big change in weather patterns. Life for many humans is likely to become much harder. Extreme weather, such as hurricanes, heat waves, blizzards, and droughts, may become more common.

B Why don't more people recycle?

Giving up greed

Long ago, the Qur'an predicted how human greed would damage the fine balance of nature:

'Evil has appeared on the land and sea because of what the men's hands have done.'

[Qur'an 30:41]

Muslims see global warming and pollution as signs from God. These signs are showing people that they cannot continue to misuse the natural world. The main cause of environmental damage is human desire for creating more wealth; more factories; more new things, quicker, faster and cheaper. Islam teaches people not to be greedy. It teaches people to remember God's wishes and to be khalifahs of the earth.

By consuming less, we can help save the environment. Muslims are taught to use what is necessary and not to waste things. The Qur'an says,

'Do not waste since God does not like the wasters.'   [Qur'an 7:31]

2 Politicians today argue about the best ways to tackle global warming. Some say all countries should reduce harmful pollution. Others say technology will solve the global warming problem and we should not put limits on energy use.

  a Which approach would you agree with? Explain your answer.

  b Would Muslim views be different to yours? Look back at Muslim views of science on pages 22–23 to help with your answer.

3 There are four really good ways of being better stewards of the environment, called the four Rs:

● **Reduce** the amount we consume.

● **Reuse** things rather than just throw old or unfashionable stuff away.

● **Recycle**, for example paper, cardboard, plastics, glass, metals.

● **Repair** things that are broken rather than just binning them.

Copy and complete table **C** with ideas of ways your school could do more to Reduce, Reuse, Recycle and Repair.

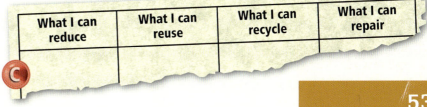

What I can reduce	What I can reuse	What I can recycle	What I can repair

C

The IFEES

objective

to be able to describe the work of an Islamic conservation organisation and to suggest your own views on its work

glossary

Conservation
Imam
Madrasah

The Islamic Foundation for Ecology and Environmental Sciences (IFEES) is the first established Muslim organisation to raise awareness of the Islamic view of the need for **conservation**. The organisation believes that it is putting into practice God's instruction that humans are to be guardians of the planet.

The organisation was formed in the mid 1980s and believes that the increasing pollution in the world, and increasing damage to the environment means that Muslims must act to overcome these problems. The projects funded by IFEES include:

- research into the causes of environmental problems and possible solutions
- producing teaching materials, books and journals
- the setting up of an experimental centre focusing on land use and organic farming and also the development of alternative technology.

The organisation is developing projects worldwide to express Islamic environmentalism in the modern world. It is engaged in many different types of projects, including:

1 spreading knowledge of Islamic environmentalism to different developing countries to help local communities protect their environment from pollution and degradation

2 encouraging local governments in developing countries to protect the environment better and live up to their environmental responsibilities as Muslim community leaders

3 educating local people themselves about Islam and environmentalism, so they learn about why they should look after the natural resources around them

4 protecting local areas from particular pollution or deforestation problems by replanting and setting up protected zones.

1 In groups, use the Internet to research *one* of the projects supported by IFEES. Find out:

a in which country the project is taking place

b what the project is hoping to achieve

c what the project involves.

Report your findings back to the class and the challenges the IFEES is facing.

People in the Sahel need wood for fuel, but cutting down trees causes desertification.

Unlike in the West, not many people know about environmental issues in developing countries. Their lives are often too hard and precarious to take on extra worries about the effect their actions are having on the environment around them.

For example, one of the IFEES's projects is based in the Sahel region at the bottom of the Sahara desert. The desert is spreading into what used to be more fertile areas because local people are cutting down all the trees and brushwood for fuel and are overgrazing their livestock on the sparse grass. Once the vegetation is gone, there is nothing to hold the soil together and it blows away in the wind.

Another key problem around the world is greed and corruption by local and national governments. This is a big problem where there are valuable resources around, like tropical forest, for example. Worldwide, an area of forest the size of a football pitch is cut down every second, and the money from the timber rarely goes to local people. While local officials get rich on the profits, local people suffer from landslides (because trees are no longer keeping the soil on slopes), and pollution in their rivers and water sources.

Islamic ethics

The IFEES hopes that it can do more than most to tackle these key problems where the people involved are Muslims. Despite care for the environment being stressed so much through the Qur'an, many Muslims in developing countries do not know how important stewardship is for doing as God wishes. So the IFEES does a lot of work spreading this knowledge to local people and to local officials.

The second part of IFEES's work is to show people how to put Islamic beliefs into practice and protect the environment around them. The way this is done is to empower local communities, including mosques, **imams** and **madrasah** teachers with the skills to protect local environments themselves.

'If the total period of life on this planet is compared to a single year, the human species has existed on it for less than 12 hours on the final day. In the brief time we have spent on this earth, we are causing the extinction of species that have lived on this planet far longer than us. It is not far-fetched to say that we are also creating conditions that put the survival of the human species itself at great risk.'

(Quote from IFEES)

Activity

2 a Following the work of the IFEES, produce a leaflet for use by development agencies in Muslim countries that explains why local people should look after the environment around them.

b Focus on *one* of the following problems: deforestation; river pollution; overfishing; or desertification. Explain why local people should care about these problems and what they could do to help prevent them.

c Make sure your leaflet uses quotes from the Qur'an and Ahadith to back up your arguments.

Jihad: struggle against injustice

objective

to be able to explain the meaning of different kinds of jihad and to compare your understanding of jihad with media use of the term

glossary

Jihad
Makkah
Soul

Muhammad's struggle

When Muhammad started preaching in his home city of **Makkah**, many of the people living there were pagans, believing in different gods. As the number of Muhammad's followers increased, so did the hostility of the pagans against him. Muhammad was physically attacked and verbally abused many times. However, he refused to hit back. Some of his followers were also beaten and tortured. Again, Muhammad advised them to be patient.

After 13 years of bitter persecution, Muhammad migrated to the city of Madinah. Here, he built the second mosque in Islam and organised his new community. But the pagans of Makkah did not leave him in peace. They attacked his new community.

Muslims were now settled in Madinah. When they were attacked, they believed God gave them permission for the first time to fight back. The Qur'an told them:

'Permission is given to those who have been attacked unjustly to fight back, God has power to give them victory.'

(Qur'an 22:38)

The Qur'an goes on to say that if God had not permitted people to defend themselves, then there would be no churches, mosques or synagogues left standing.

Different kinds of Jihad

This permission to fight is called **Jihad**. Jihad means to struggle against evil to fulfil God's wishes. Diagram **A** shows different forms of Jihad in Islam.

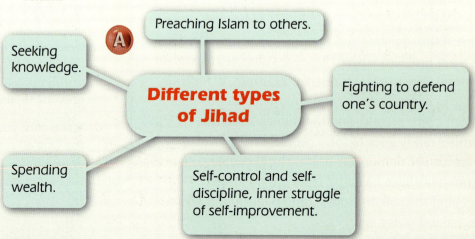

A
Preaching Islam to others.
Seeking knowledge.
Different types of Jihad
Fighting to defend one's country.
Spending wealth.
Self-control and self-discipline, inner struggle of self-improvement.

Jihad is in two parts: the Greater Jihad and the Lesser Jihad.

The Greater Jihad

Muhammad was returning home from a battle and said, 'We are returning from the Lesser Jihad to a Greater Jihad'. What Muhammad meant was that it is easy to fight an outside enemy but much more difficult to fight the enemy inside us: the enemy of greed, lust and anger. The whole life of a Muslim is a continuous Jihad, as she or he struggles to live according to God's will. The Greater Jihad is the inner battle to purify the **soul**. This includes showing a caring attitude to others.

 The Gulf War, 1991.

'On the day when every soul will be confronted with all the good it has done, and all the evil it has done, it will wish it were a great distance between it and its evil.'

(Qur'an 3:30)

1 What do you think this passage above is teaching Muslims about the way they must live their lives?

2 a From what you have read so far in this book, list *four* actions that you think a British Muslim teenager could do to please God.

  b List *four* things that you think a Muslim teenager should avoid if they do not want to go against the will of God.

Who can call for war?

Jihad as a war can only be declared by a government or ruler of a country. No individual or group can declare Jihad. If it is necessary to go to war, then it is only the rulers of the Muslim country who can decide that it is the last resort, because all other attempts to solve the dispute have failed. Even when a ruler or government goes to war, then it is expected that the rules of a just war are kept.

The Lesser Jihad

The Lesser Jihad is about going to war. The rules about going to war are very strict. The Qur'an states that war:
- is only allowed in self-defence, to protect the country
- must be the last resort after all other ways to make peace have been tried
- must not be fought to try to capture other people's lands, or for greed or ambition
- must not be used to force other people to become Muslims
- must not be fought out of hatred or anger
- must not cause any harm to innocents or non-combatants or damage natural resources.

The Qur'an says:

'Fight in God's way those who fight against you, never start hostilities. God does not like transgressors.' (Qur'an 2:190)

3 The first Gulf War (1991) happened after the Muslim country Iraq invaded the oil-rich Muslim country of Kuwait. Why do you think that many Muslim countries joined Western forces to help Kuwait regain its independence?

4 Many newspapers in Britain use the word Jihad to mean literally 'holy war'. This is not what Jihad really means. Write a short article for a national tabloid newspaper explaining in simple terms what the real meaning of Jihad is in Islam. You could use the headline: 'Why the world needs Greater Jihad'.

Moving from conflict to peace

objective

to be able to relate Islamic teachings on controlling conflict to your own experience

Someone has just pushed in front of you in a queue. The referee has given a penalty against your team for no reason. Whether it's an argument with your classmate or a driver cutting in front of your Mum's car, conflict is a part of daily life. Maybe it is becoming more and more a part of our lives, as modern lifestyles get more stressful and fast-paced. But conflict is extremely harmful: it breaks up friendships; hurts people; and causes stress and distress. Perhaps we all need to get better at managing the stress and conflict in our lives.

The Qur'an teaches Muslims that, 'Peace is better'. The Muslim greeting is, 'Peace be with you'. In fact, the word Islam comes from the word for peace. So building peace in people's lives and society is a major goal of Islam.

A One of the most common Muslim prayers says:
'O Lord you are peace,
From you comes peace
And to you returns peace
O Lord keep us alive in peace
Enter us into your house of peace.'

B

Ostrich: Denies conflict.

There's no problem.

Lemming: Keeps peace at all costs.

I'll give in coz I need you.

Gorilla: Overpowers.

You must believe me because I'm right!

Sheep: Goes with the group.

Baaa! Whatever you lot say......

Donkey: Dogmatic, judgemental, self-righteous.

I am right, you are wrong.

Owl: Hides feelings.

I think, I think, I think.

1 **How do you manage conflict? Look through the options in B and pick the description that best suits you. Describe how effective it is and think about how you could manage conflict better.**

Global issues: conflict

Controlling conflict

A lot of conflict is caused by people getting angry. Anger often feels uncontrollable – it boils up inside and feels like it has to come out or you'll explode! But Muslims are told that God wants people to control their anger and reduce the conflict that comes from it. The Qur'an says:

'Those who overcome anger and forgive people, God loves such righteous people.'

(Qur'an 3:134)

Muhammad taught his followers how to deal with anger. His message was not to get angry in the first place but he recognised that this sometimes wasn't that easy! He gave these pieces of advice:

- 'If you get angry try to be silent.'
- 'If one of you gets angry while he is standing let him sit down, if he is still angry let him lie down.'
- 'Anger is from the devil, the devil is made from fire and fire is extinguished by water, so if you become angry… [go and] wash yourself.'

> **Activity**
>
> 2 With a partner or in groups, role-play *three* situations that put Muhammad's tips on controlling anger into practice. After each one, feed back to the group on how well you think it would work for you in controlling conflict in your life.

Working for peace

Islam teaches that people should not only avoid conflict, they should also work to bring about peace. Muslims do not believe that living in peace means doing nothing. For Muslims, there are three major parts to the concept of peace: These are:

1 finding inner peace and harmony in one's own life
2 living in peaceful communities
3 seeking to overcome tension and conflict so that peace is restored.

1 Inner peace and harmony

Islam teaches that if people have no inner peace and harmony in their lives, then there will not be peace in the world, as individuals will end up in conflict with others. Muslims are taught that such inner peace and harmony comes through faith in God. Part of this faith is knowing that God has created a whole universe that moves in harmony according to his will. Islam teaches that human beings are responsible for their actions and inner peace will come if people live their lives according to God's will. People should try to fit in with this, not fight against it.

> **Activity**
>
> 3 All the things in picture **C** are forbidden in Islam. Why do you think Muslims consider that these things do not bring peace into an individual's life?

2 Living in peaceful communities

Muslims are to live in peace with each other and to help those in need. Muhammad said, 'A believer is one from whom people feel secure as regards their lives and property.'

> **Activity**
>
> 4 Outline a report for your local police force suggesting ways of reducing tension and conflict in your community.

3 Overcoming tension and conflict

Many Muslims work to overcome the causes of tension and conflict in the world. They believe that they not only have a duty to their local community, but the whole world. One famous Muslim, Yusuf Islam, said:

> It seems that conflict and natural disasters are occurring around the world in even greater frequency with a more lasting impact... We all share a responsibility to try and do whatever we can, however little, to help every victim recover from such devastating events and rebuild for the future, God willing.

Terrorism and Islam

objective

to be able to explain what terrorism is and compare different views on terrorism and to compare Islamic teachings on violence with terrorist actions

glossary

Martyr
Terrorism

Terrorism is when people use violence to frighten or intimidate populations or governments into doing what they want. Terrorists often claim that they are forced to act as they do, because it is the only way to remove what they see as an evil political or religious system.

On September 11 2001 a group of terrorists flew planes into the World Trade Centre in New York and the Pentagon building in Washington DC. Because these terrorists claimed to be Muslims, some people in the West blamed Islam – even though there is nothing in Islam as a religion that could support such an appalling act.

Islam teaches that the right to live in peace is a fundamental human right. In Islamic teaching, therefore, terrorism is totally unacceptable

Terrorism in Northern Ireland in the 20th century had religious connections. Yet no one blamed Catholic Christianity for the IRA's actions, or Protestant Christianity for Loyalist terrorism. So why is it that some people in the West think Islam is a violent religion, and that it is to blame for terrorism?

A Second plane crashing into the Twin Towers, 11 September 2001.

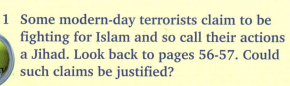

1   Some modern-day terrorists claim to be fighting for Islam and so call their actions a Jihad. Look back to pages 56-57. Could such claims be justified?

2   The right to live in peace was set out in the constitution of the first Islamic state, set up after Muhammad and his followers fled persecution in Makkah.

   ● What does persecution mean?

   ● If people are being persecuted, is it ever right for them to turn to terrorism as a way to fight back?

3   How do you feel if you are accused of doing something that was nothing to do with you?

   ● Write down the different emotions you might feel.

   ● Now write down the ways you could try to set the record straight. Which would be the most effective, if your view?

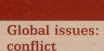

Suicide bombers

Suicide bombers are terrorists who die along with their victims in a terrorist attack. The attack on the USA on September 11 2001 was a suicide bombing, with passenger planes acting as the bombs. Britain suffered its first mainland suicide bomb attack in July 2005.

Again, suicide bombing is often wrongly linked to Islam. A person who is killed while struggling against evil in a Jihad is called a **martyr**, a shahid in Arabic, which means 'witness to the truth'. Muslims believe that all martyrs go straight to paradise because all their sins are forgiven.

While some terrorist groups claim all their suicide bombers go to paradise, Islam actually teaches that a person who commits suicide is not a martyr. Those who commit suicide are believed to go to hell. Some scholars would say that self-sacrifice can be justified in very extreme circumstances. If a person has no other way to defend themselves, are facing certain death anyway, and are able to help others survive by sacrificing themselves, then self-sacrifice can be justified. This could not apply to a terrorist attack.

B Result of the suicide bombings in London, 7 July 2005.

4 Muslims across Britain strongly condemned the 7 July 2005 London bombings, as they had September 11th, and described them as against Islam. Look over the last six pages on conflict. Prepare a list of points supporting the view that suicide bombings are un-Islamic.

C Terry Waite was held hostage by a terrorist group in Beirut for nearly five years. He now works to help victims of suffering all over the world.

At the heart of Islam, you know there lies mercy and compassion.

5 Read the following extract from the Qur'an:

'If anyone slew a person – unless it be for murder or for mischief in the land – it would be as if he slew the whole people. And if any one saved a life, it would be as if he saved the life of the whole people.'

(Qur'an 5:34–36)

a What do you think this passage is teaching?

b Why do you think many Muslim scholars use this passage to condemn acts of terrorism?

c Could a Muslim ever be justified in committing what some call 'acts of terrorism'?

Assessment for Unit 3

Once when the Prophet Muhammad and his companions were on a long journey; they came to a clear stream. It was a hot day and Muhammad's companions were tired and dusty and they went straight over to the stream and splashed about in it. But Muhammad just took a bowl from his pack and scooped up a small amount of water to wash with. His followers were amazed and asked him why. Muhammad replied 'Who gave us these good gifts but God and he gave enough for all, but we should only take what we need and not be wasteful.'

These questions test different sets of skills in RE. Which skills do you need to work on? Choose the level you need and work through the tasks set.

Level 3

- The Qur'an teaches that animals and plants are gifts from God. Do you think we have a right to use animals as we like? What are the reasons for your view?
- Newspapers often translate the Muslim term 'jihad' as meaning 'holy war'. Give a better description of what jihad means to a Muslim.
- Money from zakah (almsgiving) can only be spent on specific causes. Would you be more likely to give to some charities than others? Which charities would you support most, and why?

Level 4

- Describe what Muslims mean when they speak of being khalifahs or stewards of the earth. What difference could it make to the way they behave? Do you think it is worth doing? Why?
- Explain the difference between Greater Jihad and Lesser Jihad. Show what links them.
- Muslims believe in following God's will for people. How has this belief inspired Muslim charities to work to help others? Is this different from the way non-religious organisations, like Barnado's for example, are inspired to help those in need?

Level 5

- Many stories of Muhammad's life are about his kindness to animals and Islamic law recognised animals' legal rights centuries before animal rights organisations started in the west. Explain why the natural world is so respected in Islam. Do you think this respect for animals should be extended to the practice of sacrificing sheep at Hajj?
- What are the rules of Lesser Jihad? Do you think these laws are acceptable reasons to go to war? Does everyone have a duty to fight for their country if the cause is right? Explain your answer.
- The 20 richest people in the world own more than the 48 poorest countries in the world. Do you think anything should be done about this? What might a Muslim reply to this question?

Level 6

- Many Muslims would say there is nothing wrong with being very rich, as long as rich people fulfil the duties of zakah. Would you expect religious people to have a different attitude, and give up everything they have to the poor? What might a rich Muslim reply to this point?
- The tabloid media in this country tends to link Islam to terrorism. What aspects of Islam does this approach ignore? What reasons might newspaper owners give for making this link?
- Explain why some environmentalists use Muhammad's teachings to support radical changes in the way we exploit natural resources. What are the strengths and weaknesses of their arguments, given that Muhammad lived 1400 years ago, in a very different culture?

Glossary

Allah The Islamic word for God in the Arabic language

Atheist Someone who does not believe that God exists

Bible The holy book of Christianity

Big Bang The theory that the universe began with a giant explosion

Conservation Activities carried out to preserve the environment

Dominion Power or control over other people or things

Eid-ul-Fitr The celebration to mark the end of fasting in Ramadan

Evolution The theory that life on earth gradually developed over a long time

Fitrah The natural state of being godly and god-conscious

Global warming The increase in the temperature of the earth's surface caused by the burning of fossil fuels and pollutants

Greenhouse effect The theory that more CO_2 in the atmosphere stops heat escaping from the planet – acting like a greenhouse and warming things up

Hadith The actions, sayings and reports about the prophet Muhammad

Hajj The visiting of holy sites in Makkah and carrying out of certain rites during five days of the Hajj month

Ihram The state pilgrims enter into during Hajj when some normally permitted actions are made out of bounds for Muslims. Also the name of the simple clothing worn during Hajj

Imam The man who leads the congregation in prayer

Islamiat Islamic studies consists of studying: Islamic law, morals, prayers and biography of the Prophet

Jihad The constant struggle against any evil and injustice; and effort to do good

Jinn A creation made from fire that is intelligent and accountable.

Ka'bah A cube-shaped structure in the centre of the grand mosque in Makkah. The first house built for the worship of the one true God.

Khalifah Humans as representative of God on Earth

Madrasah A school for studying Islamiat

Mahr The dowry, a gift that the groom gives to the bride at the time of marriage

Makkah The holy city in Saudi Arabia which houses the Ka'bah

Martyr A person who dies for a noble and just cause and goes to paradise

Mosque A public building dedicated for the daily congregational and Friday prayers

Qur'an The holy book revealed by God to the prophet Muhammad

Ramadan The ninth month of the Islamic lunar calendar. Muslims fast throughout this month from just before dawn until sunset.

Resurrection Being raised from death

Sadaqah Voluntary payment or good action for charity

Salah The five daily prayers

Sawm Fasting from just before dawn until sunset.

Shahadah The declaration of faith; 'I bear witness there is no God but Allah and Muhammad is the prophet and servant of God".

Sirah Biographical writings about the conduct and example of the Prophet Muhammad

Soul The part of a person which is eternal and independent of the body

Sunnah The way of Muhammad, his practice, habit or recommendations

Surah A chapter of the Qu'ran. There are 114 chapters in all

Tawhid The belief in the oneness of God

Terrorism Attempts to change politics through terrifying people

Torah The Jewish holy book

Ummah The world-wide community of Muslims; the nation of Islam

Wudu A ritual of washing before salah

Zakah Purification of wealth by payment of annual welfare due. Annually giving 2.5 per cent of savings to the poor and needy.

Index